WHAT IS THE
WORLD COMING TO...

WHAT IS THE WORLD COMING TO..

Get the unfiltered truth, TODAY!

AARON JOHNSON

XULON PRESS

Xulon Press
2301 Lucien Way #415
Maitland, FL 32751
407.339.4217
www.xulonpress.com

Paperback ISBN-13: 978-1-66283-413-4
Hard Cover ISBN-13: 978-1-66283-414-1
Ebook ISBN-13: 978-1-66283-415-8

To my God-fearing mother, Bennie Johnson,

*Who faithfully trained up her four children
in the way they should go*

&

To my hardworking father, the late Adell Johnson,

*Who provided well for his family and instilled
in us a strong work ethic*

CONTENTS

WARNING!

1. This book is the most succinct and straightforward book you will ever read on the subject of the end times.

2. You'll find it to be both engaging and informative.

3. It's replete with tasty topics and vitamin verses to make one spiritually healthy and wise.

4. Bible prophecy is given to save the wayward sinner and stabilize the worrying saint in a "fallen" world.

5. This book is not palatable for all people.

6. This book may be inappropriate for young atheists and agnostics.

7. After reading this book, you will fall more in love with our Savior.

Read at your own risk or reward.

PREFACE

Without question, **the world is passing away, and the lust thereof, but he who does the will of God abides, forever** (1 John 2:17). And even though the world will get worse before it gets better, we (Christians) should never fear or fret. According to GOD's Word, we will live forever and outlast the world. This truth is my dominant thrust for writing this book.

My objective is to properly interpret, explain and apply scripture as it relates to biblical prophecy and the ensuing world events. Like the Apostle Paul, I **desire that the saints might be filled with the knowledge of His will in all wisdom and spiritual understanding; That we might walk worthy of the Lord unto all pleasing, being fruitful in every good work, and increasing in the knowledge of God** (Colossians 1:9,10). And, if after reading this book, it's recommended to a searching sinner, and that sinner is saved, this sacrifice and labor of love will be worth all the effort. In the words of Paul, **for though I be free from all men, yet have I made myself servant unto all, that I might gain the more . . . I am made all things to all men, that I might by all means save some** (1 Cor. 9:19, 22b).

Writing this book was a DIVINE mandate because I don't think anyone has ever publicized the insight given to me on the subject of the end times. Therefore, I insisted that this book be UNFILTERED and UNEDITED by any "smarter than God" liberals.

Thy words were found, and I did eat them; and thy word was unto me the joy and rejoicing of mine heart (Jer. 15:16).

Here are my two mandates:

1) **For though I preach the gospel** (write this book), **I have nothing to glory of: for me necessity is laid upon; yea, woe is unto me, if I preach not the gospel** (or don't write this book). I Corinthians 9:16).

2) **But as it is written, Eye hath not seen, nor ear heard, neither have entered into the heart of man, the things which God hath prepared for them that love Him. But God hath revealed them unto us by His Spirit: for the Spirit searches all things, yea, the deep things of God. For what man knows the things of a man, save the spirit of man which is in him? Even so the things of God knows no man, but the Spirit of God. Now we have received, not the spirit of the world, but the spirit which is of God; that we might know the things that are freely given to us of God. Which things also we speak, not in the words which man's wisdom teaches, but which the Holy Ghost teaches; comparing spiritual things with spiritual.** (1 Cor. 2:9-13). Since the best interpreter of Scripture is Scripture, my second mandate is to simply allow GOD to explain Himself regarding key Bible verses on the subject of eschatology.

My goal is to enable readers to **"read in the book in the law of God distinctly, and give the sense, and caused them to understand the reading"** (Neh. 8:8).

ACKNOWLEDGEMENTS

Those who know me know that I have three favorite actors: Denzel Washington, Al Pacino and Robert De Niro. And because I just love being untraditional and unorthodox at times, I decided to acknowledge Denzel because of his unique encounter with a reporter, and Robert and Al because of their character roles in two of my favorite movies.

Just recently, a young reporter asked Denzel Washington what he thought about fake news. And Denzel replied, "if you don't read the newspaper, you're uninformed. If you read the newspaper, you're misinformed." WOW! What a STRAIGHT-UP response to confound that young reporter and expose him to the deceit that is flagrantly perpetrated by mainstream and social media!

Regarding Al Pacino, I think "The Devil's Advocate" was way before its time as it exposed the Devil's insidious ways that would proceed gradually, subtly, harmfully, and ultimately, DEADLY. During a few scenes, I was spellbound because Hollywood not only exposed the devil's character, but also peeped inside his playbook. The Bible warns us: **The thief comes not, but for to steal, and to kill, and to destroy** (John 10:10a), and then admonishes us: **Be sober, be vigilant; because your adversary**

the devil, as a roaring lion, walks about, seeking whom he may devour (1 Peter 5:8).

Concerning Robert De Niro, we movie-goers know that "The Godfather" was an all- time classic. And De Niro's role as a shrewd mafia leader, aptly portrays the [behind the scene] wealthy globalists' actions of our day.

I will also like to acknowledge my three favorite prominent people: Billy Graham, Rush Limbaugh & Donald Trump.

I extol the late Billy Graham for the giant footprint he left for spreading the gospel of Jesus Christ and faithfully evangelizing the lost on such a large scale. What a severe blow he dealt to the kingdom of darkness!

To speak about the legendary Rush Limbaugh (better known as America's #1Anchor Man), I can only say, What a gift! What humor! What political insight! What business acumen! What love for Country!

And concerning Donald Trump, the best word I can give to describe him is COURAGEOUS! It took a lot of courage for him to fight for the American people as he faced relentless opposition from both Republicans and Democrats. Even their cheerleaders [the mainstream and social media] stayed on the attack even unto this day. His "America First" policies were so effective to the extent that globalists and their "Steal the election" adherents COULD NOT fathom a Trump 2nd term. For this reason, their agenda IS NOT to "Make America Great Again" or "Keep America Great", but to reduce America to a lesser nation which will keep them on their trajectory towards a One World Government.

Whether you are alive today or has "departed to be with Christ" (Phil. 1:23), I say to all six of you, Thank You!

INTRODUCTION

Q. Who could possibly know what the world is coming to?

A. Only GOD

Declaring the end from the beginning, and from ancient times the things that are not yet done, saying, My counsel shall stand, and I will do all my pleasure (Isaiah 46:1).

Thus says the Lord, the King of Israel and His Redeemer, the Lord of hosts: I am the First and I am the Last; besides Me, there is no God. Who is like Me? Let him [stand and] proclaim it, declare it, and set [his proofs] in order before Me, since I made and established the people of antiquity. [Who has announced from of old] the things that are coming? Then let them declare yet future things. Fear not, nor be afraid [in the coming violent upheavals]; have I not told it to you from of old and declared it? And you are My witnesses! Is there a God besides Me? There is no [other] Rock; I know not any (Isaiah 44:6-8 Amplified).

For all our days are passed away in thy wrath: we spend our years as a tale that is told (Ps. 90:9).

The short answer to "what the world is coming to" can be summarized in three verses:

The wicked shall be turned into hell, and all the nations that forget God (Psalm 19:7).

The kingdoms of this world are become the kingdoms of our Lord, and of His Christ; and He shall reign for ever and ever – The Millennium (Rev. 11:15)

And I saw a new heaven and a new earth: for the first heaven and the first earth were passed away; and there was no more sea --The Eternal State (Rev. 21:1).

The playbook to "what the world is coming to" can largely be found in the book of Revelation. If anyone ignores the book of Revelation, it would be impossible for that person to know the truth about eschatology. ESCHATOLOGY is the study about the end of world history, and the final destiny of the soul and of humankind. The book of Revelation "gives the sense" to Old Testament prophecies, reveals the Conquering Glorious Christ and describes His eternal program. The proper interpretation of the book of Revelation allows us to see what was formerly hidden, and to comprehend what's often mysterious. This unveiling is possible only because of the ministry of the Holy Spirit: **Howbeit when He, the Spirit of truth, is come, He will guide you into all truth: for He shall not speak of Himself; but whatsoever He shall hear, that shall He speak: and He will shew you things to come** (John 16:13).

As such, if I'm able to "give the sense, and cause you to under-standing the reading" (Neh. 8:8), we can altogether thank GOD for the Holy Spirit's anointing (John 14:16,17; 1 John 2:27).

Q. Why should we read both the Old Testament and the New Testament?

A. The Old Testatment is the New Testament concealed. The New Testament is the Old Testament revealed.

OUTLINE

Pre-Rapture Preparation Ready, Set! What is the world coming to.. Rapture (1 Thes. 4:13-18, 2 Thes. 2:1-12)

The Seven Seals (A Preview of Coming Attractions) Rev. 6

Tribulation (Matt. 24:3-14)

Gog & Magog Invasion of Israel (Ezek. 38, 39)

War in Heaven (Rev. 12:7-9)

Great Tribulation (Matt. 24:15-28)

Armageddon & The Restructured Earth (Rev. 16:12-21)

The Fall of Babylon [The World System] (Rev. 18)

World War III (Rev. 19:11- 21; 20:1-3)

1

PRE-RAPTURE PREPARATION

Needless to say, the world is going crazy. On March 31, 2021, Counterfeit News Network CNN's Cole wrote, "It's not possible to know a person's gender identity at birth, and there is no consensus criteria for assigning sex at birth."

This is just one example of outlandish statements and misbeliefs that are precursors to 2 Thes. 2:11,12. **And for this cause God shall send them strong delusion, that they should believe a lie. That they all might be damned who believed not the truth, but had pleasure in unrighteousness.**

What is truth? **And ye shall know the truth, and the truth shall make you free** (John 8:32). Today we have his truth, her truth, your truth, my truth, their truth & even our truth. What is truth? Truth is whatever GOD has said. **Sanctify** (set apart) **them through thy truth: thy word is truth** (John 17:17). Hence 'And you shall know what GOD has said, and knowing what GOD has said, shall make you free from all fear, worry and anxiety,' especially as it relates to the ensuing worldwide upheavals.

WORLD OVERCOMERS

The Bible (GOD's Word) declares **"For whatsoever is born of God overcomes the world: and this is the victory that overcomes the world, even our faith. Who is he that overcomes the world, but he that believeth that Jesus is the Son of God (1 John 5:4,5)? I have written unto you, fathers, because ye have known Him that is from the beginning. I have written unto you, young men, because ye are strong, and the word of God abides in you, and ye have overcome the wicked one. Love not the world, neither the things that are in the world. If any man loves the world, the love of the Father is not in him. For all that is in the world, the lust of the flesh** (pleasure), **and the lust of the eyes** (possession), **and the pride of life** (power), **is not of the Father, but is of the world. And the world passes away, and the lust thereof: but he that does the will of God abides forever (1 John 2:14-17).**

Interpretation: It's natural for unbelievers to love the world and cling to the things that are in the world because they believe the world is all there is to explore and enjoy. And when world events and conditions go awry, unbelievers commonly fear, fret, freak out and even "sorrow as people which have no hope."(1 Thes. 4:13b). Scripture declares **'There is no peace, says the Lord, unto the wicked"** (Isa. 48:22). However, for Christians to respond in "like fashion" is very sad and embarrassing to the kingdom of GOD. Scripture is very clear that Christians will live forever and outlast the world. Even today, (during the

2020-2021 pandemic) it's unfortunate how many Christians would go everywhere, but to church; We would talk and listen to everyone, but GOD; We would read everything but the Bible. Even many pastors, teachers and preachers would address everything but GOD's word in their sermons. And we wonder why most (but not all) Christians fail to **"fight the good fight of faith, and lay hold on eternal life."** (I Tim. 6:12). PLEASE UNDERSTAND! There are only two things that are eternal on planet earth --that being, human beings and GOD's Word. We humans may try, but we can never take what's "temporal" to satisfy what's eternal. **He that loves silver shall not be satisfied with silver; nor he that loves abundance with increase: this is also vanity** (futility/chasing the wind). Eccl. 5:10

For those who operate as if the Bible and the church are irrelevant, please note:

THE BIBLE IS MORE CURRENT THAN TOMORROW'S NEWSPAPER & THE CHURCH IS MORE ESSENTIAL THAN THE LOCAL GROCERY STORE.

For our days are passed away in thy wrath: we spend our years as a tale that is told (Ps. 90:9). And why do I say the church is more essential? Consider John 4:31-34 **Meanwhile His disciples urged Him, "Rabbi eat something. But He (Jesus) said to them, "I have meat to eat that you know not of. Therefore said the disciples one to another, "Could someone have brought Him food? Jesus said unto them, My meat is to do the will of Him that sent Me, and to finish His work** Matthew 4:1-4 is another companion text for us to prioritize nourishing the inner man with GOD's Word just the same way we would feed the outer man (natural body) with food. I encourage you to read Matt. 4:1-4 as soon as possible. If you're too busy and think procrastination is a better option, then YOUR PROBLEM IS NOT YOUR PROBLEM; YOUR WRONG RESPONSE IS YOUR PROBLEM.

Smarter than GOD

There is a way that seems (appears, feels) **right unto a man, but the end thereof are the ways of death** (Prov. 14:12). Without question, the secular world we live in today promotes rebellion against GOD and against civil authority. They have determined that no one should have the right to control anyone's behavior. As a result, GOD's word warns that they **"later shall receive to themselves damnation"** (Romans 13:2b). Isaiah 5 identifies and warns the "smarter than GOD" unbelievers: **Woe to those who call evil good and good evil, who put darkness for light and light for darkness, who put bitter for sweet and sweet for bitter. Woe to those who are wise in their own eyes and clever in their own sight. Woe to those who are heroes at drinking wine and champions at mixing drinks, who acquit the guilty for a bribe, but deny justice to the innocent. Therefore, as the tongues of fire lick up straw and as dry grass sinks down in the flames, so their roots will decay and their flowers blow away like dust; for they have rejected the law of the Lord Almighty and spurned the word of the Holy One of Israel** (vss. 20-24 NIV).

And without question, the unbelievers are not alone. Christian apathy will also be common (especially in the last days) to be akin to **"seeds which fell among thorns; and the thorns sprung** up, **and choke them"** (Matt. 13:7). Jesus explains, **He also that received seed among the thorns is he that hears the word; and the care of this world, and the deceitfulness of riches, choke the word, and he becomes unfruitful** (Matt. 13:22). Mark 4:19 further adds, **"and the lusts of other things entering in, choke the word, and it becomes unfruitful."**

Now for those Christians who are smarter than GOD, who know it all, who are too busy to read or study GOD's word, who willfully and habitually duck and dodge Bible study, who continuously sit under a ministry where sermons offer one opening scripture, followed by storytelling . . . if that's YOU, you no longer have to live in defeat, worry about tomorrow or blame others for your problems, pain and grief. The Bible offers a sure remedy: **And wisdom and knowledge shall be the stability of thy times, and strength of salvation: the fear of the Lord is his treasure** (Isa. 33:6).

SELF- STUDY

Today we no longer have to wait until Sunday to be spiritually fed. The prophet encourages us to **"seek ye out of the book of the Lord, and read"** (Isaiah 34:16). Notice scripture says "read," and not "read and try to understand." Whenever we mark out a time to **"give attendance to reading, to exhortation, to doctrine** (1 Tim. 4:13), GET READY FOR THE DEVIL TO SHOW UP! He will whisper in your ear, "You don't have time today." If you read the Bible, you won't understand it, so why bother? Moreover, at this moment in time, you're very busy and have a lot going on. So you should read the Bible later. [And we all know the drill: We have many places to go and people to see]. And, if that's not the case, the devil will convince you that you're really tired, and you know you will fall asleep the moment you start reading it. Finally, we acquiesce... ok, tomorrow, tomorrow... and the devil leaves GRINNING until the next time you have those (out of this world) thoughts to read the Bible.

In the words of the late Iona Locke, "a backwards, ignorant saint is a joy to the enemy. What we don't know, can hurt and will destroy us." GOD's word is clear: **My people are destroyed for lack of knowledge: because thou hast rejected knowledge, I will also reject thee, that thou shalt be no priest to me: seeing thou hast forgotten the law of thy God, I will also forget thy children** (Hosea 4:6). So, Watch Out & Be Careful! BIBLICAL IGNORANCE CAN BE BOTH DEBILITATING & GENERATIONAL.

DARE TO READ THE BIBLE

But for those of us who dare to **"to give attendance to reading, to exhortation, to doctrine** (Timothy 4:13), in the words of King David, we will declare **"O how love I thy law! It is my meditation all the day. Thou through thy commandments hast made me wiser than mine enemies: for they are ever with me. I have more understanding than all my teachers: for thy testimonies are my meditation. I understand more than the ancients, because I keep thy precepts"** (Ps. 119:97-100).

To be candid, I personally attend church to enter into GOD's corporate presence and to fellowship with the saints. If I receive a word from the sermon, I consider that a BONUS. And it's because I, like the Apostle Paul, **"desire to be filled with the knowledge of his will in all wisdom and spiritual understanding"** via personal study (Colossians 1:9). And there are plenty others who DON'T DEPEND ON OTHERS FOR SPIRITUAL NOURISHMENT. When we arrive at church, oftentimes, we come with our minds and hearts already filled with GOD's Word from personal study. Remember the verse, **"But the Anointing which ye have received of Him abides in you, and ye need not that any man teach you: but as the same Anointing teaches you of all things, and is truth, and is no lie, and even as It hath taught you, ye shall abide in Him"** (1 John 2:27).

Personal Bible reading is key to **"walking in the light"** or "being in the know"(1 John 1:7). And when we just dive into God's word, we often experience that the understanding will come as we allow the Holy Spirit to lead and guide us into all truth. Again, **"Howbeit when He, the Spirit of truth, is come, He will guide you into all the truth. For He shall not speak of Himself, but whatever He shall hear, that shall He speak. And He will shew you things to come"** (John 16:13). In other words, the Holy Spirit will connect the scriptures for you **"because it is given unto you to know the mysteries of the kingdom of heaven, but to them** (the unbelievers**) it is not given** (Matt. 13:11). Thus every Christian has the DIVINE mandate to **study to show thyself approved unto God, a workman does not need to be ashamed, rightly dividing the word of truth** (2 Tim. 2:15).

ENCOURAGE GOD's MINISTERS

"I charge thee therefore before God, and the Lord Jesus Christ, who shall judge the quick and the dead at His appearing and His kingdom, Preach the word; not your opinion, the nightly news, prominent people, or today's politics, but PREACH THE WORD, be instant in season, out of season; reprove, rebuke, exhort with all longsuffering and doctrine. For the time will come when they will not endure (tolerate) sound doctrine; but after their own lust shall they heap to themselves teachers, having itching ears (for something pleasing and gratifying); And they shall turn away their ears from the truth, and shall be turned unto fables" (myths) 2 Timothy 4:2-4.

Again, WHAT IS TRUTH? TRUTH IS WHATEVER GOD HAS SAID. "The prophet that hath a dream, let him tell a dream; and he that hath my word, let him speak my word faithfully. What is the chaff to the wheat? Says the LORD. Is not my word like as a fire? Says the LORD; and like a hammer that breaks the rock in pieces" (Jer. 23:28,29)? ONLY GOD's WORD CAN IGNITE THE MINDS, NOURISH HUNGRY SOULS AND PENETRATE HARD HEARTS. Today, the GOD of Heaven & Earth is telling us ministers: Be not afraid of their faces: for I am with thee to deliver thee, says the LORD (Jeremiah 1:8). And when opposition comes, here's the perfect prayer: And now, Lord, behold their threatenings: and grant unto thy servants, that with all boldness they may speak thy word, By stretching forth thine hand to heal; and that signs and wonders may be done by the name of Thy holy child Jesus (Acts 4:29,30).

REMEMBER THE DEVIL USUALLY GETS THE BEST SEAT AT MOST CHURCH SERVICES. But we are instructed to **"let both wheat and tares grow together until the harvest: and in the time of harvest I will say to the reapers, Gather ye together first the tares, and bind them in bundles to burn them: but gather the wheat into my barn** (Matt. 13:30).

APPRECIATE GOD'S MINISTERS

As every man hath received the gift, even so minister the same one to another, as good stewards of the manifold grace of God. If any man speak, let him speak as the oracles (utterances) **of God; if any man minister, let him do it as of the ability which God gives: that God in all things may be glorified through Jesus Christ, to whom be praise and dominion for ever and ever. Amen** (Peter 4:10,11).

PLEASE NOTE a revelation I received from the teaching ministry of Andre Carrington:

Speaking gifts are divided among 4 anointing characteristics: 1) Revelation 2) Knowledge 3) Prophesying 4) Doctrine

Now, brethren, if I come unto you speaking with tongues, what shall I profit you, except I shall speak to you either by revelation, or by knowledge, or by prophesying, or by doctrine (1 Corinthians 14:6)?

Hence my anointing happens to be dual -- that being, a combination of revelation & doctrine. "Revelation" simply means that I reveal GOD's Word, which is His Will, and through "Doctrine"

I show you where to find it. GUESS WHAT? I'm no better than the ministers who would "Prophesy" or those ministers who provide much "Knowledge". Notably, most mega church pastors, Christian radio & television ministers have the anointing characteristic of "Knowledge" coupled with a small ounce of "Doctrine" with the exception of the late Adrian Rogers, the late Dr. Vernon McGee, Richard Caldwell, Tony Evans, Robert Jeffers, David Jeremiah, Charles Stanley, Ed Young, John Mac Arthur, Jr. and a few others whose anointing characteristics are that of "Knowledge" and "Doctrine." However, when we consider T.D. Jakes and I.V. Hilliard, their anointing characteristics are that of "Knowledge" and "Revelation." This is not a judgment, but an observation! However, for those Christians who like to judge and compare ministers, GOD says, **GROW UP!**

And I, brethren, could not speak unto you as unto spiritual, but as unto carnal, even as unto babes in Christ. I have fed you with milk, and not with meat: for hitherto ye were not able to bear it, neither yet now are ye able. For ye are yet carnal: for whereas there is among you envying, and strife, and divisions, are ye not carnal and walk as men. For while one says, I am of Paul; and another, I am of Apollos; are ye not carnal? Who then is Paul, and who is Apollos, but ministers by whom ye believed, even as the Lord gave to every man (1 Cor. 3:1-5)? INTERPRETATION: If a certain minister is boring and puts you to sleep, there's nothing wrong with that minister or you, it simply means that you either had a rough night or you aren't assigned to his/her ministry. GOD gives to every believer a minister. And when that minister speaks, the believer assigned to that minister comes alive, and hangs on his/her every word, **even as the Lord gave to every man** (1 Cor. 3:5).

Therefore, YOUR FAVORITE OR PREFERRED SPEAKER IS GOD'S ASSIGNED MINISTER TO YOU. **I have planted, Apollos watered; but God gave the increase. So then neither is he that plants anything, neither he that waters; but God that gives the increase. Now he that plants and he that waters are one** (and on the same team)**: and every man shall receive his own reward according to his own labor** (and there's no need for division, envy or jealousy). **For we are laborers together with God: ye are God's husbandry, ye are God's building** (1 Cor. 3:6-9). In other words, WE ARE NOT CRABS IN A BUCKET. Whether a certain minister is your favorite or your least favorite, appreciate him or her for their work and labor of love. **Now this I say, that every one of you says, I am of Paul; and I of Apollos; and I of Cephas; and I of Christ. Is Christ divided** (1 Cor. 1:12, 13a)? LET'S APPRECIATE ALL OF GOD's MINISTERS.

Two More Preps Before Exploring This Incredible Journey Into Eschatology

1. The Theology Test

Theology is the study of GOD.

For every word below, write in the direct opposite of that word.

Hot _____

Up _____

In _____

GOD _____

If you wrote in Devil, Satan or Lucifer for GOD's direct opposite, you scored 75 on the overall test, but made a ZERO and failed the theology portion of the test.

GOD HAS NO DIRECT OPPOSITE. Never compare a creature with THE CREATOR. Remember GOD is eternal and self-existing, having no beginning or end.

Before the mountains were brought forth, or ever thou had formed the earth and the world, even from everlasting to everlasting, thou art God (Psalm 90:2).

Satan, the god of this world will remain on GOD's leash, until he and his angels are cast into hell. Thus Satan (The Supreme God –Hater) knows what his eternal destiny holds. He has determined that if he and his homeys (the fallen angels) are headed to hell, they won't go alone. He will blind the minds of many who **"walk according to the course of this world, according to the prince of the power of the air** (namely the airwaves of radio, television, mainstream and social media), **the spirit who now works in the children of disobedience** (Eph. 2:2). "The course of this world" says what you see is what you get; there is no afterlife. No heaven. No hell. Therefore, live it up. Pursue every pleasure. Chase any evil. Just do what's right in your own eyes because when you're dead, you're DONE. Yet I remind you that **the devil is a liar, and the father of it** (John 8:44).

2. BIBLE STUDY TIPS FOR BEGINNERS

1) Preferably read from a Bible that offers reference scriptures.

2) In the Old Testament, read the Psalms and Proverbs, first. These 2 books will whet the appetite and provide a panoramic view about life issues and how the scriptures relate.

3) In the New Testament, start with the gospel of John to capture the life and ministry of Jesus Christ as the Son of GOD.

2

READY, SET! WHAT IS THE WORLD COMING TO..

Of all the 66 books of the Bible, Satan has used only the book of Revelation to frighten and discourage GOD's people from reading it. Yet Revelation is the only book where scripture says **"Blessed is he that reads, and they that hear the words of this prophecy, and keep those things which are written therein: for the time is at hand** (Revelation 1:3). "For the time is at hand" means that nothing else now has to occur before the Rapture and the beginning of the Tribulation Period.

KUDOS, JOHN MACARTHUR, JR

He describes the Book of Revelation to be "a rich source of truth about eschatology; in fact, it contains more details about the end times than any other book of the Bible. Revelation portrays Christ's ultimate triumph over Satan, depicts the final political setup of the world system, and describes the career of the most powerful dictator in human history, the final Antichrist. It also mentions the Rapture of the church (3:10) and describes the seven-year time of Tribulation, including the three and one-half years of the Great Tribulation (7:14; cf. Matt. 24:21), the second coming of Christ, the climactic battle of human history (Armageddon), the thousand-year earthly kingdom of Jesus Christ, the final judgment of unrepentant sinners (the Great White Throne judgment), and the final state of the wicked in hell (the lake of fire) and the redeemed in the new heaven and new earth" (The MacArthur New Testament Commentary, Revelation 1-11, page 2).

THE KEY VERSE

The key verse to unlock the mystery and properly interpret the book of Revelation can be found in Rev. 1:19: Jesus (Our Resurrected Lord) tells the Apostle John to **"write the things which thou hast seen , and the things which are, and the things which shall be hereafter."** "The things which thou hast seen" is Revelation chapter 1 which reflects the PAST. "The things which are" is Revelation chapters 2 and 3 which reflect the PRESENT. This is the church age. Notably, THE CHURCH AGE BEGAN AT PENTECOST AND WILL END AT THE RAPTURE OF THE CHURCH. "And the things which shall be hereafter" is chapters 4 – 22 which reflect the FUTURE. However, Rev. 22:6-21 returns to GOD's message for the present age.

Today, Christians will continue to live in the PRESENT (Revelation chapter 2 & 3) until we are raptured (snatched away or vanish from the earth).

RAPTURE (THE LORD'S COMING) DESCRIBED IN TWO PASSAGES OF SCRIPTURE

1) **But I would not have you to be ignorant, brethren, concerning them which are asleep** [a euphemism for "dead"], **that ye sorrow not, even as others which have no hope. For if we believe that Jesus died and rose again, even so them also which sleep in Jesus will God bring with Him. For this we say unto you by the word of the Lord, that we which are alive and remain unto the coming of the Lord shall not prevent** (precede) **them which are asleep. For the Lord Himself shall descend from heaven with a shout, with the voice of the archangel, and with the trump of God: and the dead in Christ shall rise first: Then we which are alive and remain shall be caught up together with them in the clouds, to meet the Lord in the air: and so shall we ever be with the Lord. Wherefore comfort one another with these words** (1 Thes. 4:13-18).

2) **Now we beseech you, brethren, by the coming of our Lord Jesus Christ, and by our gathering together unto Him, That you be not soon shaken in mind, or be troubled, neither by spirit, nor by word, nor by letter as from us, as though the day of Christ had come. Let no man deceive you by any means: for that day shall not come, except there come a falling away first, and that man of sin be revealed, the son of perdition;** [This is the beast out of the sea (Rev. 13:1), the little horn (Dan

7:8), and the false Christ which is the Antichrist who will aim to rule the world (Rev. 13:15-17). This is the Antichrist]. **Who opposes and exalts himself above all that is called God, or that is worshiped; so that he as God sits in the temple of God, showing himself that he is God** (2 Thes. 2:4). This parallels the "abomination of desolation" (Matt. 24:15; cf. Dan. 9:27; 11:31; 12:11) During the Great Tribulation (second 3 ½ years), the Antichrist will desecrate the rebuilt temple in Jerusalem, and usurp worship for himself.

Do you not remember that when I was yet with you, I told you these things? And now you know what withholds (restrains) **that he might be revealed in his time. For the mystery of iniquity** (lawlessness) **is already at work: only He** (The Holy Ghost/ The Sin Restrainer) **Who now restrains will do so, until He is taken out of the way. And then shall that wicked** (Antichrist) **be revealed, whom the Lord shall consume with the spirit** (breath) **of His mouth, and shall destroy with the brightness of His coming: Even him** (the False Prophet), **whose coming is after the working of Satan with all power and signs and lying wonders, and with all deceivableness of unrighteousness in them that perish; because they received not the love of the truth, that they might be saved. And for this cause God shall send them strong delusion, that they should believe a lie: That they all might be damned** (condemned) **who believed not the truth, but had pleasure in unrighteous** (2 Thes. 2:1 - 12).

Two Observations Regarding the Antichrist

1) The church will be in heaven and never experience the tyranny of the Antichrist on earth. For this reason, THE ANTICHRIST WILL NOT BE REVEALED UNTIL AFTER THE RAPTURE OF THE CHURCH (2 Thes. 2:7,8).

2) SATAN (HIMSELF) DOESN'T KNOW WHO THE ANTICHRIST WILL BE. He also must wait until after the Rapture to find out! The Bible explains, **"Little children, it is the last time: and as you have heard that antichrist shall come, even now are there many antichrists; whereby we know that it is the last time** (1 John 2:18). Ever since Jesus Christ rose from the dead and returned to be with the Father, scripture is clear: Many antichrists will appear in subsequent generations. However, the capital "A" Antichrist will be the ultimate opponent of GOD to thwart His plan and destroy His people—that being, namely the unbelieving Jews who dwell on the earth after the Rapture. Scripture refers to this period of time as "THE TIME OF JACOB's TROUBLE, but he shall be saved out of it" (Jer. 30:7).

Israel's Blindness, Consolation & Restoration

The GREAT TRIBULATION will be the unprecedented worst time to live on planet earth. Nonetheless, Israel will be saved from it: **For I would not, brethren, that ye should be ignorant of this mystery, lest ye should be wise in your own conceits; that blindness in part is happened to Israel, until the fullness of the Gentiles be come in. And so all Israel shall be saved: as it is written, There shall come out of Zion the deliverer, and shall turn away ungodliness from Jacob. For this is my covenant unto them, when I shall take away their sins. As concerning the gospel, they are enemies for your sakes: but as touching the election, they are beloved for the fathers' sakes** (Romans 11:25-28).

Now here's a teaser to be found in Revelation 12:13: **And when the dragon** (Satan) **saw that he was cast unto the earth, he persecuted the woman** (Israel) **which brought forth the man child** (Jesus). **And to the woman were given two wings of a great eagle, that she might fly into the wilderness, into her place, where she is nourished for a time, and times, and half a time** (3 ½ years), **from the face of the serpent** (Rev. 12:13,14). WHAT A THRILLER TO BE DISCUSSED FURTHER IN CHAPTER 6!

WHY THE RAPTURE?

The Rapture will surely occur due to one certain biblical principle: GOD WILL NOT DESTROY THE RIGHTEOUS WITH THE WICKED. In Genesis 18, Abraham intercedes for Sodom and Gomorrah: **And Abraham drew near, and said, Wilt thou also destroy the righteous with the wicked? Peradventure there be fifty righteous within the city: wilt thou also destroy and not spare the place for the fifty righteous that are therein? That be far from Thee to do after this manner** to slay the righteous with the wicked: and that the righteous should be as the wicked, that be far from thee: Shall not the Judge of all the earth do right? And the Lord said, If I find in Sodom fifty righteous within the city, then I will spare all the place for their sakes (Gen. 18:23-26). Bible readers know the rest of the story; Abraham's intercession started from 50, then to 45, 40, 30, 20, 10. And the Lord went His way, as soon as He had left communing with Abraham: and Abraham returned unto his place (vs. 33). Then the Lord rained upon Sodom and upon Gomorrah brimstone and fire from the Lord out of heaven; And He over threw those cities, and all the plain, and all the inhabitants of the cities, and that which grew upon the ground (Gen. 19:24,25).

Scripture even explains why GOD destroyed the two cities: And the Lord said, because the cry of Sodom and Gomorrah is great, and because their sin is very grievous (Gen. 18:20).

GOD's MODUS OPERANDI is always to remove the righteous before destroying the wicked:

Much more then, being justified by His blood, we [Christians who are the bride of Christ] (cf. Rev. 21:9) shall be saved from wrath through Him (Romans 5:9).

For God hath not appointed us to wrath, but to obtain salvation by our Lord Jesus Christ. Who died for us, that, whether we wake or sleep, we should live together with Him (1 Thes. 5:9,10). This particular truth brings us to the identification of the 24 elders.

The 24 Elders

Who are they?

They are NOT 24 individuals. The number 24 is a number of representation (1 Chron. 24). Scripture clearly identifies the 24 elders as the RAPTURED CHURCH: **And when He** (Jesus) **had taken the book, the four beasts** [referring to the four living creatures which are the 4 cherubim who protect GOD's throne] **and four and twenty elders fell down before the Lamb, having every one of them harps, and golden vials full of odors, which are the prayers of** (tribulation) **saints** who yet dwell on the earth. **And they** (the 24 elders) **sung a new song, saying, Thou art worthy to take the book, and to open the seals thereof: for thou was slain, and hast redeemed us** (24 elders) **to God by thy blood out of every kindred, and tongue, and people, and nation** [to represent an astronomical number of people which is much greater than 24 individuals]. Jesus promised, **"And this gospel of the kingdom shall be preached in all the** (inhabited) **world for a witness unto all nations; and then shall the end come** (Matt. 24:14). When Jesus spoke the words, **"then shall the end come"**, He was referring to the end of the church age which began at Pentecost and will end at the Rapture. Notably, in chapter 4, this same scripture will apply during the Tribulation to once again signify that **"the Lord is longsuffering toward us, not willing that any should perish but that all should come to repentance"** (2 Pet. 3:9b).

And hast made us unto our God kings and priests: and we [the raptured church who is also the bride of Christ] **shall reign on the earth** (Rev. 5:8-10) with Christ for 1,000 years during the

Millennium. In Revelation 20:6, scripture affirms, **Blessed and holy is he that hath part in the first resurrection; on such the second death hath no power, but they shall be priests of God and of Christ, and shall reign with Him a thousand years.**

Again, the "prayers of saints" refer to the prayers of tribulation saints who yet dwell on the earth; **And when He** (Jesus) **had opened the fifth seal, I** (John) **saw under the altar the souls of them that were slain for the word of God, and for the testimony which they held: And they** [referring to the tribulation saints who died and immediately appeared in heaven](cf. 2 Cor. 5:8) **cried with a loud voice, saying, How long, O Lord, holy and true, dost thou not judge and avenge our blood on them that dwell on the earth? And white robes were given unto every one of them; and it was said unto them, that they should rest yet for a little season, until their fellow servants also and their brethren, that should be killed as they were, should be fulfilled** (Rev. 6:9-11).

DOES HISTORY REPEAT ITSELF?

And as it was in the days of Noah, so shall it be also in the days of the Son of man. They did eat, they drank, they married wives, they were given in marriage, until the day that Noah entered into the ark, and the flood came, and destroyed them all. Likewise also as it was in the days of Lot; they did eat, they drank, they bought, they sold, they planted, they builded; But the same day that Lot went out of Sodom it rained fire and brimstone from heaven, and destroyed them all. Even thus shall it be in the day when the Son of man is revealed. In that day, he which shall be upon the housetop, and his stuff in the

house, let him not come down to take it away: and he that is in the field, let him likewise not return back. Remember Lot's wife. Whosoever shall seek to save his life shall lose it; and whosoever shall lose his life shall preserve it (Luke 17:26-33).

INTERPRETATION: It's easy to be saved TODAY! After the church is raptured, SALVATION WILL COST YOU YOUR VERY LIFE.

But what saith it? The word is nigh thee, even in thy mouth, and in thy heart: that is, the word of faith, which we preach; That if thou shalt confess with thy mouth the Lord Jesus, and shalt believe in thine heart that God hath raised Him from the dead, thou shalt be saved. For with the heart man believes unto righteousness; and with the mouth confession is made unto salvation. For the scripture says, whosoever believes on Him shall not be ashamed. For there is no difference between the Jew and the Greek: for the same Lord over all is rich unto all that call upon Him. FOR WHOSOEVER SHALL CALL UPON THE NAME OF THE LORD SHALL BE SAVED. How then shall they call on Him in whom they have not believed? And how shall they believe in Him of whom they have not heard? And how shall they hear without a preacher? And how shall they preach, except they be sent? As it is written, *How beautiful are the feet of them that preach the gospel of peace, and bring glad tidings of good things* (Romans 10:9-15).

HISTORY DOES NOT REPEAT ITSELF! However, flesh is flesh. Scripture explains: **For to be carnally** (worldly) **minded is death; but to be spiritually minded is life and peace. Because** the carnal mind is enmity against God: for it is not subject to the law of God, neither indeed can be. So then they that are in the flesh cannot please God. But ye are not in the flesh but in the Spirit, if so be that the Spirit of God dwell in you. Now if any man have not the Spirit of Christ, he is none of His (Romans 8:6-9).

THE HOLY GHOST?

WHERE IS THE HOLY GHOST, TODAY? Scripture reveals that the Holy Ghost indwells every believer. In John 14:15-20, we read, **if ye love me, keep my commandments. And I will pray the Father, and He shall give you another Comforter, that He may abide with you forever, Even the Spirit of truth: whom the world cannot receive, because it sees Him not, neither knows Him: but ye know Him; for He dwells with you, and shall be in you. I will not leave you comfortless: I will come to you. Yet a little while, and the world sees Me no more; but you see Me: because I live, ye shall live also. At that day** (of death or Rapture), **you shall know that I am in the Father, and you in Me, and I in you.**

REMEMBER I Thes. 4 14: **For if we believe that Jesus died and rose again, even so them also which sleep** (physically died) **in Jesus will God bring with Him.** That means JESUS WILL NOT BRING DEAD SAINTS WITH HIM. To be ABSENT from the body is to be gloriously PRESENT with the LORD (2 Cor. 5:8 paraphrased) as light beings. Daniel 12:3 reminds us: **And they that are wise shall shine as the brightness of the firmament; and they that turn many to righteousness as the stars forever and ever.**

You cannot bury a child of God.

In Luke 16:19-31, Jesus differentiates what happens upon the sinner's death vs. what happens upon the saint's death. Verses 22 and 23 read: **And it came to pass, that the beggar** (Lazarus) **died, and was carried by angels into Abraham's bosom: the rich man also died, and was buried; And in hell he lift up his eyes, being in torments, and sees Abraham afar off, and Lazarus in his bosom.** Please note here that ONLY THE SINNER IS BURIED, AND NOT THE SAINT. It's quite interesting to hear some ministers say, "I'm glad that I am on top of the ground, and the ground is not on top of me." And the congregation will usually chuckle in agreement. Nonetheless, such an ignorant statement may be catchy, but is definitely unbiblical.

Scripture further points to another Lazarus who was sick and died, leaving his two sisters, Mary and Martha, to mourn and become very distraught. In John 11, Jesus purposely arrives late, knowing that He would raise Lazarus from the dead. Now let's continue reading verses 21 – 26. **Then said Martha unto Jesus, "Lord, if thou had been here, my brother would not have died. But even now I know that whatever You ask of God, God will give You." Jesus said unto her, "Your brother will rise again." Martha said to Him, "I know that he will rise again in the resurrection at the last day."**

Notably, I refer to Martha's response as THE MARTHA SYNDROME. It's an opinion that has been considered the truth among most Christians throughout generations. Most Christians believe that they will see their loved ones "again in the resurrection at the last day." **Jesus said to her, "I am the resurrection and the life. He who believes in Me, though he were dead, yet shall he live. And whoever lives and believes in Me shall never die. Do you believe this?'**

Even today, regarding the (physical) death of Christian loved ones, Jesus yet ask the question, what do YOU believe? Will you believe Martha's opinion, or MY WORD?

2 Cor. 5:1,6-8 confirm **"For we know that if our earthly house of this tabernacle** (physical body) **were dissolved, we have a building of God, a house not made with hands, eternal in the heavens .. therefore we are always confident, knowing that, whilst we are at home in the body, we are absent from the Lord: (For we walk by faith, not by sight:) We are confident, I say, and willing rather to be absent from the body, and to be present with the Lord.** Again, WE ARE ETERNAL LIGHT BEINGS. Daniel 12:3 will affirm, **"And they that be wise shall shine as the brightness of the firmament; and they that turn many to righteousness as the stars for ever and ever."**

Knowing this particular truth, I have never cried at the funeral of a loved one, and don't think I ever will because I completely believe GOD's word on the subject matter regarding physical death. DON'T MISUNDERSTAND ME! I am far from being callous and cold-hearted. I also have moments of tears. At this point in time, I have never cried at a loved one's funeral.

Here's a question for you: WHEN DOES FOREVER BEGAN?

If you will ponder that question for just a moment, as a Christian, YOU WILL NEVER FEAR DEATH or **sorrow, even as others which have no hope** (cf. 1 Thes. 4:13b).

When considering The Transfiguration recorded in Matt. 17:1-9, Mark 9:1-10, and Luke 9:28-36, these passages (all the more) affirm Jesus' statement **"and whoever lives and believes in Me shall never die.** SO WHAT'S THE POINT? Moses and Elijah appeared on planet earth as eternal light beings and could be readily identified by Peter, James, and John. GUESS WHAT? If you or I had witnessed Jesus' Transfiguration, the Father could have easily sent one of our loved ones back to earth in whom we would readily recognized as a light being. (Of Course we would immediately hit the deck to avoid blindness). Scripture is emphatic: **For He is not the God of the dead, but of the living, for all live unto Him** (Luke 20:38). WHETHER A PERSON IS IN HEAVEN OR HELL, ALL LIVE UNTO HIM.

And when Christians die, we instantly appear in heaven as eternal light beings and are happier than we've ever been. Scripture is very clear: **Blessed are the dead which die in the Lord from henceforth** [and now on]. **"Yes", says the Spirit, that they may rest from their labors** [done on earth], **and their works** [of obedience] **do follow them (Rev. 14:13).** And to be duly noted, "rest from their labors" DOES NOT REFER TO SOUL SLEEP. Eternal light beings don't require rest.

The Apostle Paul describes it best:

So also is the resurrection of the dead. It is sown in corruption; it is raised in incorruption: It is sown in dishonor; it is raised in glory: it is sown in weakness; it is raised in power: It is sown a natural body; it is raised a spiritual body. There is a natural body, and there is a spiritual body. And so it is written, the first man Adam was made a living soul; the last Adam was made a quickening spirit. Howbeit that was not first which is spiritual, but that which is natural; and afterward that which is spiritual. The first man is of the earth, earthy: the second man is the Lord from heaven. (AND DON'T MISS THAT)! Once again, scripture reveals that the second man is the Lord from heaven).Here's another reference scripture: **Beloved, now we are the children of God; and it has not yet been revealed what we shall be, but we know that when He** (Jesus) **is revealed, we shall be like Him, for we shall see Him as He is** (1 John 3:2). I inserted this verse parenthetically. Now, let's continue in 1 Cor. 15:48. **As is the earthy, such are they also that are earthy: and as is the heavenly, such are they also that are heavenly. And as we have borne the image of the earthy, we shall also bear the image of the heavenly. Now this I say, brethren, that flesh and blood cannot inherit the kingdom of God; neither doth corruption inherit incorruption. Behold, I show you a mystery; We shall not all sleep** (experience physical death), **but we shall all be changed** (referring to those who are still living at the time of the Rapture), **In a moment, in the twinkling of an eye, at the last trump** (1 Thes. 4:16): **for the trumpet shall sound, and the dead** (saint's physical body) **shall be raised incorruptible, and we shall be changed. For this corruptible must put on incorruption, and this mortal must put on immortality** [as eternal light beings]. **So when this corruptible shall have put on immortality, then shall be brought** to pass the saying that is written, Death is swallowed up in victory. O DEATH, where is thy sting? O GRAVE, where is thy victory? [Note: While Stephen was being stoned to death in Acts 7, he never said, OUCH! Instead, "he was calling upon God, and saying, Lord Jesus, receive my spirit. And he kneeled, down, and cried with a loud voice, Lord, lay not this sin to their charge. And when he had said this, he fell asleep (vss. 59-60)], thus leaving his physical body and departing to be with Christ, which is far better (Phil. 1:23). The Apostle Paul continues, the sting of death is sin; and the strength of sin is the law. But thanks be to God, which giveth us the victory through our Lord Jesus Christ. Therefore, my beloved brethren, be ye steadfast, unmovable, always abounding in the work of the Lord, forasmuch as ye know that your labor is not in vain in the Lord (1 Cor. 15:42-58).

PLEASE NOTE THAT THE SAINTS WILL BE CHANGED AT THE MOMENT OF PHYSICAL DEATH OR AT THE RAPTURE. There's NO PURGATORY to atone for personal sins; There's no TWILIGHT ZONE; And there's NO WAITING TO RISE AGAIN IN THE RESURRECTION AT THE LAST DAY (The Martha Syndrome).

HEAVEN'S POPULATION GROUP

To affirm that we are eternal light beings, heaven's population list can be found in Hebrews 12:22-24: **But rather, you have come to Mount Zion, even to the city of the living God, the heavenly Jerusalem, and to countless multitudes of angels in festal gathering, And to the church** (assembly) **of the**

Firstborn who are registered [as citizens] in heaven, and to
the God Who is Judge of all, and to the spirits of the righteous (the redeemed in heaven) **who have been made perfect.
And to Jesus, the Mediator** (Go-between, Agent) **of a new covenant, and to the sprinkled blood which speaks [of mercy], a
better and nobler and more gracious message than the blood
of Abel [which cried out for vengeance]** (Gen. 4:10 Amplified).
OBSERVATION: In contrast, Abel's brother (Cain) did not
make the "cut" and will remain in hell until his final sentencing
which is The Great White Throne of Judgment. Afterwards,
Cain, along with all others who have personally rejected GOD,
will be cast alive into the lake of fire (Rev. 20:4).

FREEDOM FROM FEAR OF DEATH

**Forasmuch then as the children are partakers of flesh and
blood, He also Himself likewise took part of the same; that
through death He might destroy him that had the power
of death, that is, the devil; and deliver them who through
fear of death were all their lifetime subject to bondage**
(Hebrews 2:14-15).

What is death? When applied to living things such as plants
and animals, it means the end of life. With reference to human
beings, death is not the end of life, nor the end of existence;
Death is SEPARATION.

THERE ARE 3 DEATHS:

1) SPIRITUAL DEATH is the separation of the human
spirit from God's Spirit.

And the Lord God commanded the man, saying, "of every tree of the garden thou may freely eat: but of the tree of the knowledge of good and evil, thou shall not eat of it: for in the day that you eat of it you shall surely die" (Gen. 2:16. 17). Most of us know that after the "first Adam" sinned, he immediately died (spiritually), yet he continued to live (physically).

And you hath he quickened, who were (spiritually) dead in trespasses and sins (Eph. 2:1);

> 2) PHYSICAL DEATH is the separation of the human spirit from the natural body.

For as the body without the spirit is dead, so faith without works is dead also (James 2:26). There is no man that hath power over the spirit to retain the spirit; neither hath he power in the day of death (Eccl: 8:8). Jesus is the ONLY ONE who demonstrated power in the day of death when He explained, Therefore doth my Father love Me, because I lay down My life, that I might take it again. No man takes it from Me, but I lay it down of Myself. I have power to lay it down, and I have power to take it again. This commandment have I received of My Father (John 10:17,18). When Jesus therefore had received the vinegar, He said, It is finished: and He bowed His head, and (voluntarily) gave up the ghost (John 19:30).

> 3) SOUL DEATH is the second death which is eternal separation of the soul from God.

And the devil that deceived them was cast into the lake of fire and brimstone, where the beast and the false prophet are, and shall be tormented day and night for ever and ever.. (Rev. 20:10-15). **And whosoever was not found written in the book of life was cast into the lake of fire** (Rev. 20:15).

In summary, everyone arrives on planet earth spiritually dead. **For as in Adam all die, even so in Christ shall all be made alive** (1 Cor. 15:22). Spiritual death then leads to physical death [unless we are raptured]. **Wherefore, as by one man** [referring to the first Adam] **sin entered into the world and death by sin; so death passed upon all men, for that all have sinned** (Rom. 5:12). If anyone personally rejects Jesus Christ as Lord and Savior, that person is destined to experience eternal death **"when the Lord Jesus shall be revealed in heaven with His mighty angel, in flaming fire taken vengeance on them that know not God, and that obey not the gospel of our Lord Jesus Christ: Who shall be punished with everlasting destruction from the presence of the Lord, and from the glory of His power; When He shall come to be glorified in His saints, and to be admired in all them that believe (because our testimony among you was believed) in that day** (2 Thes. 1:7-10).

SALVATION IN CHRIST ALONE

And this is the record, that God hath given to us eternal life, and this life is in His Son. He that hath the Son [living inside you] **hath life; and he that hath not the Son of God** [living inside you] **hath not life** (1 John 5:11, 12).

Jesus said unto him, I am the way, the truth, and the life: no man comes unto the Father, but by Me (John 14:6).

Neither is there salvation in any other: for there is none other Name under heaven given among men, whereby we must be saved (Acts 4:12).

For there is one God, and one mediator between God and men, the man Christ Jesus (1 Tim. 2:5).

Look unto Me, and be ye saved, all the ends of the earth: for I am God, and there is none else (Isaiah 45:22).

Therefore I said to you that you will die in your sins; for if you do not believe that I am He, you will die in your sins (John 8:24).

The Lord is nigh unto all them that call upon Him to all that call upon Him in truth. He will fulfill the desire of them that fear Him: He also will hear their cry, and will save them (Ps. 145:18, 19).

IN HIS IMAGE

In the beginning and afterwards speaking everything into existence (seen and unseen), the Trinity (GOD The Father, GOD The Son & GOD The Holy Ghost) said **"Let Us make man in Our image, after Our likeness: and let them have dominion over the fish of the sea, and over the fowl of the air, and over the cattle, and over all the earth, and over every creeping thing that creeps upon the earth. So God created man in His own image, in the image of God created He him; male and female created He them** (Gen. 1:26, 27).

In the two verses above, we find 2 simple truths:

1) Mankind was made to "work" the earth, and not "worship" the earth.

   Can someone please remind the rogue environmentalists and their tree- hugging adherents that **the world is passing away** (1 John 2:17)?

2) There are only two genders: male and female.

According to Dr. Google, there are at least 86 genders, and I dare not get into the weeds of trying to name every manufactured "concocted" gender. Suffice it to say, **Let God be true, but every man a liar** (Romans 3:4a) . . . and let's all be reminded that **God is not the author of confusion** (1 Cor. 14:33). It's very sad that we allow the Enemy to confuse the young minds of our innocent children, especially in America: The "One Nation under God"

In 1 Thes. 5:23, the Apostle Paul describes GOD's masterpiece of all creation – that being, the human's (TRIUNE) makeup: **And the very God of peace sanctify you wholly; and I pray God your whole spirit and soul and body be preserved blameless unto the coming of our Lord Jesus Christ.** PLEASE UNDERSTAND:

Spirit is WHAT we are; Soul is WHO we are; Body is WHERE we are.

Spirit is our GOD awareness; Soul is our SELF awareness; Body is our WORLD awareness.

If anyone should travel to outer space, a space suit would be required. If anyone should enter planet earth, a body would be required. The body is our earth suit. Hence the only legal entry into planet earth is through the birth canal: In order to come to planet earth, you must be born here! Or to put it aptly, YOU MUST BE SENT HERE BECAUSE WE EXISTED BEFORE WE WERE BORN. Regarding the birth of the prophet Jeremiah, Scripture is clear: **Before I formed thee in the belly I knew thee; and before thou came forth out of the womb I sanctified thee, and I ordained thee a prophet unto the nations** (Jer. 1:5). Regarding the birth of John the Baptist, scripture is also clear: **There was a man sent from God, whose name was John** (John 1:6).

Even Jesus Himself, had to legally enter planet earth through the birth canal: **Wherefore when He cometh into the world, He said, sacrifice and offering thou would not, but a body thou hast prepared me** (Heb. 10:5). Jesus further contrast His entry with Satan's entry when He said: **Verily, verily, I say unto you, he** (Satan) **who does not enter by the door** (of birth) **into the sheepfold** (as Israel's Messiah), **but climbs up some other way, the same is a thief and a robber** (John 10:1)

AS TRIUNE BEINGS,

GOD The Father relates to the spirit: **Furthermore, we have had human fathers who corrected us, and we paid them** respect. **Shall we not much more readily be in subjection to the** <u>Father of spirits</u> **and live** (Heb.12:9)?

GOD The Son relates to the body: **Wherefore when He** (Jesus) **cometh into the world, He said, Sacrifice and offering thou would not, but a body hast thou prepared Me** (Heb. 10:5). **Now ye are the** <u>body of Christ</u>**, and members in particular** (1 Cor. 12:27).

GOD The Holy Spirit relates to the soul which is comprised of our intellect, emotion and will. **And be renewed in the** <u>spirit of your mind</u>**; And that ye put on the new man, which after God is created in righteousness and true holiness** (Eph. 4:23,24).

Now with the SOUL being who we are . . . and on the bases of what we (individually) think, and how we (individually) feel, we make our (individual) choices.

GOD DOES NOT SEND ANYONE TO HEAVEN; GOD DOES NOT SEND ANYONE TO HELL. WE CHOOSE, AND GOD RESPECTS OUR CHOICE.

When Judas Iscariot, one of Jesus' twelve disciples, betrayed the MASTER for 30 pieces of silver (Matt. 26:15,16), he afterwards hanged himself (Matt. 27:5). And when Matthias replaced Judas to be **numbered with the eleven apostles,** scripture reports, **that he** (Matthias) was selected to **take part of this ministry and apostleship, from which Judas by transgression fell, that he might go to his own place** – that being, HELL, the place of his own choosing (Acts 1:25,26).

Abortion?

The thief (Satan) **comes not, but for to steal** (our possessions), **kill** (our bodies), **and to destroy** (our purpose): **I** (Jesus) **have come that they might have life, and that they might have it more abundantly** (John 10:10).

Sadly, today's abortion advocates have convinced themselves that abortion is health care, and not death care. Therefore, proper burials of slaughtered babies are not required.

WHAT IS THE TRUTH ABOUT ABORTION? Remember TRUTH is whatever GOD has said.

Here are 5 observations that today's fake news and godless academia won't tell you:

1) Children DO NOT come from having sex.
   Even though there's a whole lot of sex going on in the world, all sexual intercourse does not produce babies because CHILDREN COME FROM GOD. Jeremiah 1:5 declares, **"Before I formed you in the womb, I knew you; Before you** [came out of the womb and] **were born, I sanctified you; and ordained you a prophet to the nations."** Sex is the channel; GOD is the source. **Lo, children are an heritage of the LORD: and the fruit of the womb is His reward** (Ps. 127:3).

2) With the exception of the birth of Jesus Christ, NONE OF US CHOSE OUR PARENTS. So, who are we to decide who gets to live or die because an innocent infant

was conceived out of circumstances [of rape, incest, or even under-age parents in which] we don't approve of?

3) Abortion only stops the baby's entry into the earth, but never the baby's existence. Remember that we are eternal beings. When King David fasted and prayed for GOD to spare his newborn son . . . and the child soon died, David responded, **"But now he is dead, wherefore should I fast? Can I bring him back again? I shall go to him, but he shall not return to me"** (2 Sam. 12:23). Application: ALL CHRISTIAN MOTHERS WHO ABORTED THEIR CHILD WILL REUNITE WITH HIM/HER AGAIN IN HEAVEN. What a SURE &BLESSED HOPE!!!

4) The baby is a human being at conception, and not a "blob of tissue." Therefore, Christians should vote for only pro-life candidates. The Bible admonishes preachers and politicians to **"open their mouth for the dumb** (who cannot speak for themselves) **in the cause of all such as are appointed to destruction"** (Prov. 31:8).

5) Abortion providers should be prosecuted. The Bible is clear: **If men strive** (fight), **and hurt a woman with child, so that her fruit depart from her** (prematurely or die) **and yet no mischief follow: he shall be surely punished, according as the woman's husband will lay upon him; and he shall pay as the judges determine** (Exodus: 21:22).

It's so sad and unfortunate that many Christians have been duped on the abortion issue. Some even say, "if it is legal, it must be right!" In the words of the late Adrian Rogers, "No law can be legally right that is morally wrong." **Shall the throne of iniquity have fellowship with thee, which frames mischief by a law** (Ps. 94:20)? Exodus 20:13 aptly reminds us, **Thou shalt not kill** [or commit murder].

Book of Life

There are two applications to understand the Book of Life: First application is before the Rapture of the Church. The second application is after the Rapture of the Church. Consider

BEFORE THE RAPTURE

Everyone arrives on planet earth with a score of 100. That means that all of our sins were paid for in full: past, present and future. Consider John 1:29: **The next day John** (The Baptist) **saw Jesus coming toward him, and said, Behold! The Lamb of God who takes away the sin of the world.** DON'T MISS THAT TRUTH! Jesus took away the sins of the whole world, and not just the sins of the believers. Here's another one: **Now all things are of God, Who has reconciled us to Himself through Jesus Christ, and has given us the ministry of reconciliation, that is, that God was in Christ reconciling the world** [and not just the saints, but the whole world] **to Himself, not imputing** [and adding up] **their trespasses to them, and has committed to us the word of reconciliation. Now then, we are ambassadors for Christ, as though God were pleading through us: we implore you on Christ's behalf,**

be reconciled to God. For He made Him who knew no sin to be sin for us, that we might become the righteousness of God in Him (2 Cor. 5:18-21). These verses are aptly known as THE GREAT EXCHANGE of human sins for GOD's righteousness. Another reference passage is Romans 9:11-33. REMEMBER: God does not exact double payment for sins; We either accept Christ's payment or we pay. In the words of the timeless song, **JESUS PAID IT ALL:**

I hear the Savior say, Thy strength indeed is small; Child of weakness, watch and pray, Find in Me thine all in all."

Refrain: *Jesus paid it all, All to Him I owe; Sin had left a crimson stain, He washed it white as snow.*

For nothing good have I Whereby Thy grace to claim; I'll wash my garments white In the blood of Calv'ry's Lamb.

And now complete in Him, My robe, His righteousness Close sheltered 'neath His side, I am divinely blest.

Lord, now indeed I find Thy pow'r, and Thine alone Can change the leopard's spots And melt the heart of stone

When from my dying bed My ransomed soul shall rise, "Jesus died my soul to save" Shall rend the vaulted skies.

And when before the throne I stand in Him complete, I'll lay my trophies down, All down at Jesus' feet.

He who overcomes shall be clothed in white garments, and I will not blot out his name from the Book of Life, but I will confess his name before My Father and before His angels. He who has an ear, let him her what the Spirit says to the churches (Rev. 3:5, 6). Remember the church age began at Pentecost and will end at the Rapture. Please also note: THE ONLY WAY FOR A NAME TO BE BLOTTED OUT, IT MUST FIRST BE WRITTEN IN. Exodus 32:31-33 is another scripture reference where names were warned to be blotted out. Even in Psalms 69:19--28, David petitioned God to blot out the names of all those who participated in the crucifixion of Jesus Christ, to be removed from the Book of Life.

Thus everyone who arrived on planet earth BEFORE THE RAPTURE, has their names written in heaven. But for those individuals who personally reject Jesus Christ as Savior and Lord, scripture warns **"how shall we escape if we neglect so great a salvation"** (Heb. 2:3). And to put it more seriously, scripture further warns: **"Of how much sorer punishment, suppose ye, shall he be thought worthy, who hath trodden under foot the Son of God, and hath counted the blood of the covenant, wherewith he was sanctified, an unholy thing, and hath done despite unto the Spirit of grace? For we know Him that hath said, Vengeance Belongs Unto Me, I will recompense, says the Lord. And again, The Lord Shall Judge His People. It is a fearful thing to fall into the hands of the living God"** (Heb. 10:29-31). With that said, now we're brought to:

AFTER THE RAPTURE

And all that dwell upon the earth shall worship him (The Anti-Christ)**, whose names are not written in the book of life of the Lamb slain from the foundation of the world** (Rev. 13:8). Scripture further explains: **The beast** (The Anti-Christ) **that you saw was, and is not, and will ascend out of the bottomless pit and go to perdition. And those who dwell on the earth will marvel, whose names are not written in the Book of Life from the foundation of the world, when they see the beast that was, and is not, and yet is** (Rev. 17:8). In this case, "those whose names are not written in the Book of life" refer to those who "**received a mark in their right hand, or in their foreheads**" (cf. Rev. 13:16) during the Tribulation [first 3 ½ years] & Great Tribulation [second 3 ½ years] period which immediately followed the Rapture of the Church.

As you can see, reading the Bible can be both REVEALING & RIVETING. Keep your seat belts fastened and your eyes opened while we continue to explore this fascinating journey into eschatology.

DOCTRINE OF PREDESTINATION

If you think GOD has predestined some to go to heaven, and others to go to hell . . . my friend, you are sadly mistaken. Even the most popular Bible verses remind us: **For God so loved the world, that He gave His only begotten Son, that whoever believes in Him should not perish but have everlasting life** (John 3:16). **For God did not send His Son into the world to condemn the world, but that the world through Him might** be saved. He who believes in Him is not condemned; but he who does not believe is condemned already, because he has not believed in the name of the only begotten Son of God. And this is the condemnation, that the light has come into the world, and men loved darkness rather than light, because their deeds were evil. For everyone practicing evil hates the light and does not come to the light, lest his deeds should be exposed. But he who does the truth comes to the light, that his deeds may be clearly seen, that they have been wrought in God (John 3:16-21).

Of a truth, GOD **"wants (ALL) everyone to be saved and to come to the knowledge of the truth"** (1 Tim. 2:4). Scripture begs the question, **Have I any pleasure at all that the wicked should die? says the Lord GOD: and not that he should return from his ways, and live** (Ezek. 18:23)? **Say unto them, As I live, says the Lord GOD, I have no pleasure in the death of the wicked; but that the wicked turn from his way and live: turn ye, turn ye from your evil ways; for why will ye die, O house of Israel** (Ezek. 33:11)?

Ephesians chapter 1 covers the "doctrine of predestination "in greater detail. In that, I will address only verses 9-12: **Having made known unto us the mystery of His will, according to His good pleasure which He hath purposed in Himself. That in the dispensation of the fullness of time He might gather together in one all things in Christ, both which are in heaven, and which are on earth; even in Him: In Whom also we have obtained an inheritance, being predestined according to the purpose of Him who works all things after the counsel of His own will:**

NOW HERE'S THE CLINCHER VERSE TO THE DOCTRINE OF PREDESTINATION: **That we who first trusted in Christ should be to the praise of His glory.** In this passage, "Predestinate" means to "to mark off or choose before" who will be GOD's initial "ambassadors" for spreading the gospel on the earth. SCRIPTURE IS CLEAR: "We who first trusted in Christ" refers to the Jews of the flesh. Remember Jesus told the Samaritan woman at the well, **"You worship what you do not know; we know what we worship, for salvation is of the Jews** (John 4:22). Even Paul himself exclaimed, **"For I am not ashamed of the gospel of Christ: for it is the power of God unto salvation to everyone who believes; to the Jew first, and also to the Greek** (Romans 1:16). Thus GOD has chosen the Jews (of the flesh) first, to participate in His plan for salvation and **"reconcile others to God"** (2 Cor. 5:20).

For to this end we both labor and suffer reproach, because we trust in the living God, Who is the Savior of ALL MEN, especially of those who believe (1 Tim. 4:10). Again, GOD does not send anyone to heaven, nor does He send anyone to hell. For the most part, we choose our eternal destiny, and GOD respects our choice. The exceptions are the children, the mentally retarded or the mentally incapacitated. And why is this? It's because if any person don't have the maturity or mental capacity to accept Jesus as Lord, neither does he/she have the capacity to reject Him. Once again, Jesus is the Savior of ALL MANKIND, especially of those who believe (1 Tim. 4:10). And in His sovereignty, He predestined the Jews to be the first people group to spread the gospel of Jesus Christ throughout the world.

Don't know GOD?

Q. What about those who never knew there's a GOD?

A. They do not exist.

For the invisible things of Him from the creation of the world are clearly seen, being understood by the things that are made, even His eternal power and Godhead; so that they are without excuse: Because that when they knew God, they glorified Him not as God, neither were thankful; but became vain in their imaginations, and their foolish heart was darkened. Professing themselves to be wise, they became fools, And changed the glory of the incorruptible God into an image made like to corruptible man, and to birds, and four-footed beasts, and creeping things. Wherefore God also gave them up to uncleanness through the lusts of their own hearts, to dishonor their own bodies between themselves: Who changed the truth of God into a lie, and worshiped and served the creature more than the Creator, who is blessed forever. Amen. For this cause God gave them up unto vile affections: for even their women did change the natural use into that which is against nature. And likewise also the men, leaving the natural use of the woman, burned in their lust one toward another; men with men working that which is unseemly, and receiving in themselves that recompense which is meet. (This matter is even spelled out in our traffic signs: If anyone tries to ENTER an EXIT, that person is going the WRONG WAY). **And even as they did not like to retain God in their knowledge, God gave them over to a reprobate mind, to do those things which are not convenient; Being**

filled with all unrighteousness, fornication, wickedness, covetousness, maliciousness; full of envy, murder, debate (strife),
deceit, malignity (evil-mindedness), whisperers, backbiters,
haters of God, despiteful, proud, boasters, inventors of evil
things [including the abortion pills], disobedient to parents,
without understanding, covenant breakers, without natural affection, implacable (unforgiving), unmerciful: Who
knowing the judgment of God, that they which commit such
things are worthy of death, not only do the same, but have
pleasure in them that do them (Romans 2: 20-32).

For the grace of God that brings salvation has appeared
to ALL men, teaching us that, denying ungodliness and
worldly lusts, we should live soberly, righteously, and godly
in the present age (Titus 2:11,12). Even those who live in
the remotest regions were created in GOD's image and after
His likeness, thus having a GOD-consciousness (Gen. 1:27).
Remember "spirit" is what we are, signifying that all human
beings have a GOD-awareness.

As a matter of fact, ALL CREATION KNOWS AND
RECOGNIZES GOD. When God split the red sea, enabling
the Israelites to pass on dry ground, scripture reveals: "The
waters saw thee, O God, the waters saw thee; they were afraid:
the depths also were troubled" . . . as "You led Your people
like a flock by the hand of Moses and Aaron:" (Ps. 77:16, 20).

Even in Luke 19, we find that "the whole multitude of the disciples began to rejoice and praise God with a loud voice for all
the mighty works that they had seen; Saying, BLESSED BE
THE KING THAT COMETH IN THE NAME OF THE

LORD: peace in heaven, and glory in the highest. And some of the Pharisees from among the multitude said unto Him, Master, rebuke Thy disciples. And He answered and said unto them, I tell you that, if these should hold their peace, the stones would immediately cry out (Luke 19:37 b-40).

WHAT'S THE POINT? Because the atheists and agnostics have convinced themselves that Nothing created Everything, they all would be better off, having water for eyes, and rocks for brains. **It is a fearful thing to fall into the hands of the living God** (Heb. 10:31).

3

THE SEVEN SEALS
(A Preview of Coming Attractions)

1. White Horse will represent a temporary false peace perpetrated by the Anti-Christ (Rev. 6:2).

2. Red Horse will bring war worldwide because **"peace is taken from the earth"** (Rev. 6:3-4).

3. Black Horse will cause worldwide famine immediately following worldwide war (Rev. 6:5,6).

4. Pale Horse will bring more death and hell **"over the fourth part of the earth, to kill with the sword, and with hunger, and with death, and with the beast** (wild animals) **of the earth"** (Rev. 6:7,8).

5. Fifth Seal will be worldwide martyrdom as the Anti-Christ and his henchmen behead millions who refused to **"receive a mark 666 in their right hand, or in their**

foreheads" in order to buy or sell (cf. Rev. 13:15-18).
(Rev. 6:9-11)

6. Sixth Seal will welcome the World's Most Massive
Earthquake, with 60 – 100 lb. meteors falling to the
earth, **and causing the sky to vanish like a scroll that's
being rolled up. And every mountain and island was
removed from its place while people seek death** [in
order] **to escape GOD's wrath** (Rev. 6:12-17).

7. Seventh Seal will bring the world to Revelation 8 where
scripture records **thirty minutes of silence in Heaven
followed by thunders & lightning, and another earthquake, followed by hail and fire mingled with blood
being cast to the earth, burning up the third of trees
and green grass** (vs. 7), **followed by a third of the sea
becoming blood, as a great mountain burning with
fire was cast into it** (vs 8), **destroying a third of sea
creatures and a third of ships** (vs. 9), **including a third
of rivers and fountains of water** (vs. 10). **And the third
part of the** (fresh) **waters became Wormwood, causing
many to die from the bitter waters** (vs.11), **and a third
part of the sun, moon and stars were all smitten,
causing them not to shine a third part of day and a
third part of the night** (vs. 12). Verse 13 announces
more woes to the inhabitants of the earth because THE
WORST IS YET TO COME.

HOW TOUGH ARE YOU?

To all the big, bad, and tough guys who just love their sin, shake their fists at God, and declare, "We don't need a Savior . . . and boastfully say, this is my life and no one (including Jesus) can tell me how to live it." Interestingly enough, this personality type will be among the very ones portrayed in Revelation 6:15-17: **And the kings of the earth, and the great men, and the rich men, and the chief captains, and the mighty men, and every bondman, and every free man, hid themselves in the dens** [caves] **and in the rocks of the mountains; And said to the mountains and rocks, Fall on us, and hide us from the face of Him who sits on the throne, and from the wrath of the Lamb: For the great day of His wrath is come; and who shall be able to stand?** Now here's the point, Gentlemen. Testosterone is good. However, when it's mixed with arrogance and stupidity, it can later become regretfully deadly. So prior to meeting your Maker face to face, I gladly offer each of you "tough ones" a slice of "humble" pie before that terrifying day. It's quite nutritional and well known for regulating the heart (cf. Prov. 23:26) and renewing the mind (cf. Rom. 12:2). Some of you can thank me later.

HELL ON EARTH

In Rev. 9, the bottomless pit (the abyss which is the abode for the worst demons) is opened, and smoke rose from it, causing the sun and sky to darken (vs. 2). [Smoke from the "pit" indicates fires below], signifying that hell is NOT a state of mind. In this scene, locust-like creatures come out of the smoke (vs. 3) **and they were commanded that they should not hurt the grass,**

neither any green thing, neither any tree; Now here's a short reprieve for the rogue environmentalists and their tree-hugging earth worshippers. They will have a picnic and experience brief satisfaction, but not for long. Scripture continues, **but those men which have not the seal of God in their foreheads, to them** (referring to the most vile demons) **it was given that they should not kill them, but that they should be tormented five months: and their torment was as the torment of a scorpion, when it strikes a man** (vss. 4,5). Because the demons are not allowed to kill anyone at this point, scripture reports, **and in those days shall men seek death, and shall not find it; and shall desire to die, and death shall flee from them** (Rev. 9:6).

That even means if someone attempted suicide by jumping from the Empire State Building, upon crashing, the skull may be busted, the body would be broken in pieces, blood and guts may be scattered, yet that person will continue to breathe and suffer unthinkable pain. And to add INSULT TO INJURY, the "scorpion-like stinging" by these indestructible demons will continue [even if the unbelievers were wearing masks and got vaccinated] until the five months have ended. And that's how much the Devil and his demons hate you. Mask or No Mask! Vaccination or No Vaccination! Broken or Unbroken!

Following this, the next judgment will be even worse. The four most wicked demons which were bound by GOD in the great river Euphrates, were released (vss.14, 15) to kill a third of the world's population. These four demons will be in charge over 200,000,000 demons that are referenced as "the army of the horse men" (vs. 16). **And thus I saw the horses in the vision, and them that sat on them, having breastplates of fire, and** of jacinth, and brimstone: and the heads of the horses were as the heads of lions; and out of their mouths issued fire and smoke and brimstone. By these three was the third part of men killed, by the fire, and by the smoke, and by the brimstone, which issued out of their mouths. For their power is in their mouth, and in their tails: for their tails were like unto serpents, and had heads, and with them they do hurt (Rev. 9:17-19).

DEPTH OF DEPRAVITY

And the rest of the men which were not killed by these plagues yet repented not of the works of their hands, that they should not worship devils, and idols of gold, and silver, and brass, and stone, and of wood: which neither can see, nor hear nor walk: Neither repented they of their murders, nor of their sorceries, nor of their fornication, nor of their thefts (Rev. 9: 20, 21). Can you believe that? The very ones who defy the God of the Bible will become all the more religious, and less righteous. Murder, drug use, sexual immorality and thefts will be the unrestrained, addictive activities and ORDER of that day.

THE 144.000 SEALED

According to Wikipedia, the Jehovah's Witnesses believe that exactly 144,000 faithful Christians will be in heaven. They do not believe in predestination or eternal security. They believe in different forms of resurrection for two groups of Christians: One group, the anointed (144,000) go to heaven while the other group, "the other sheep" or "the great crowd" will live forever on earth.

WHAT HOGWASH! Scripture clearly identifies the 144,000 as twelve thousand men from each of the twelve tribes of Israel: **And I** (John) **heard the number of them which were sealed: and there were sealed a hundred and forty and four thousand of all the tribes of the children of Israel** (Rev. 7:4). Of the tribe of Judah, Rueben, Gad, Asher, Naphtali, Manasseh, Simeon, Levi, Issachar, Zebulun, Joseph and Benjamin, were each sealed twelve thousand (Rev. 7:5-8). And, as a result of their worldwide evangelism, a numberless multitude was saved (out of the tribulation on earth) and joined us in heaven (vs. 9). **And one of the elders answered, saying unto me, What are these which are arrayed in white robes? And whence came they? And I said unto him, Sir, thou knowest. And he said to me, These are they which came out of great tribulation, and have washed their robes, and made them white in the blood of the Lamb.** [Having physically died during the Tribulation &Great Tribulation] **Therefore are they before the throne of God, and serve Him day and night in His temple: and He that sits on the throne shall dwell among them. They shall hunger no more, neither thirst any more; neither shall the sun light on them, nor any heat** [because they left the earth]. **For the Lamb which is in the midst of the throne shall feed them, and shall lead them unto living fountains of waters: and God shall wipe away all tears from their eyes** (Rev. 7:13-17).

According to Jehovah's Witnesses, perhaps the Apostle John was delusional when he said **"I saw a new heaven and a new earth: for the first heaven and the first earth were passed away; and there was no more sea** (Rev. 21:1). How can the majority of them live forever on earth, and 144,000 faithful ones only occupy heaven? Scripture is so clear: **the first heaven and the**

first earth shall pass away; and there will be no more sea (cf. Rev. 21:1)

Please understand that to live on the "first earth", every living creature requires water to survive. NO WATER. NO LIFE. NO SURVIVORS. However, having "glorified" bodies, water will not be essential to sustain life because HEAVEN IS NOW! Heaven is not tomorrow; Heaven is not future; Heaven is not past. Heaven is now. Do you remember HEAVEN'S POPULATION GROUPS? **But ye are** (now) **come unto mount Zion, and unto the city of the living God, the heavenly Jerusalem, and to an innumerable company of angels, To the general assembly and church of the first-born, which are written in heaven, and to God the Judge of all, and to the spirits of just men made perfect. And to Jesus the mediator of the new covenant, and to the blood of sprinkling, that speaks better things than that of Abel** (Heb. 12:22-24). BOTTOMLINE: HEAVEN'S POPULATION IS COUNTLESS, AND NOT JUST 144,000.

For this reason, scripture admonishes us to avoid Jehovah's Witnesses or any group of people whose doctrine rejects the Bible, which is GOD's Word: Scripture is emphatic:

Whosoever transgresses and abides not in the doctrine of Christ, does not have God. He that abides in the doctrine of Christ, has both the Father and the Son. If there come any unto you, and bring not this doctrine, receive him not into your house, neither bid him Godspeed. For he that bids him Godspeed is partaker of his evil deeds (2 John 1:9-11).

Reading this scripture reminds me of The Million Man March in Washington D.C. on October 16, 1995. Louis Farrakhan called for a large gathering of African-American men to march around the National Mall. [Of course, as a Christian, I could care less about attending any event promoted by a Jew-hater or Christ-blasphemer]. However, prior to the event, on April 11, 1994, Farrakhan was allowed to speak to a large crowd of men at the Pleasant Grove Baptist Church, a large iconic black membership church which is located in the Fifth Ward community of Houston, TX. Of course, I wouldn't think of being in the very vicinity for such an event, let known, attend such flagrant heresy. Nevertheless, since that event, the church membership teetered downwardly, and never recovered. It's so unfortunate that the late Charles Jackson did not heed these very applicable verses. The Word is so clear, and it bears repeating for the sake of any church pastor who would invite or allow any person who does not abide in the doctrine of Christ to address the congregation where he's appointed the under Shepherd.

Whosoever transgresses and abides not in the doctrine of Christ, does not have God. He that abides in the doctrine of Christ, has both the Father and the Son. If there come any unto you, and bring not this doctrine, receive him not into your house, neither bid him Godspeed. For he that bids him Godspeed is partaker of his evil deeds (2 John 1:9-11).

THE 2 WITNESSES

In Revelation 11, GOD will also give power unto His 2 witnesses who will prophesy during the Great Tribulation which is the second 3 ½ years of the total seven years (vs. 3). **And** if any man will hurt them, fire proceeds out of their mouth, and devours their enemies: and if any man will hurt them, he must in this manner be killed (vs. 5). Interpretation: There is BAD breath; Then there is DEADLY breath. These (two) have power to shut heaven, that it rain not in the days of their prophecy: and have power over waters to turn them to blood, and to smite the earth with all plagues, as often as they will. And when they shall have finished their testimony, the beast (Antichrist) that ascended out of the bottomless pit shall make war against them, and shall overcome them, and kill them. And their dead bodies shall lie in the street of the great city, which spiritually is called Sodom (referring to its lewdness and immorality) and Egypt (depicting oppression and bondage), where also our Lord was crucified (Jerusalem). And they of the people and kindreds and tongues and nations shall see their dead bodies three days and a half, and shall not suffer their bodies to be put in graves (WHAT INDIGNITY!). And they that dwell upon the earth shall rejoice over them, and make merry, and shall send gifts one to another; because these two prophets tormented them that dwelt on the earth. And after three days and a half the Spirit of life from God entered into them, and they stood upon their feet; and great fear fell upon them which saw them. And they heard a great voice from heaven saying unto them, Come up hither. And they ascended up to heaven in a cloud; and their enemies beheld them [as GOD vindicates their message]. And the same hour was there a great earthquake, and the tenth part of the city fell, and in the earthquake were slain of men seven thousand: and the remnant [those who are not killed by the earthquake] were affrighted, and gave glory to the God

of heaven. The second woe is past; and behold, the third woe cometh quickly (vss. 6-14).

Remember The Seven Seals are a preview of coming attractions. They will play out after the church is raptured, and is dwelling in heaven.

4

TRIBULATION
(Matt. 24:3-14)

"And as he sat upon the mount of Olives, the disciples came unto him privately, saying, Tell us, when shall these things be? And what shall be the sign of thy coming, and of the end of the world? And Jesus answered and said unto them, Take heed that no man deceive you. For many shall come in my name, saying, I am Christ; and shall deceive many. And ye shall hear of wars and rumors of wars: see that ye be not troubled: for all these things must come to pass, but the end is not yet. For nation shall rise against nation, and kingdom against kingdom: and there shall be famines, and pestilences, and earthquakes in divers (various) places. All these are the beginning of sorrows (or birth pangs coming more frequently with more intensity). Then shall they deliver you (unbelieving Jews and tribulation Saints who refuse to receive the "mark 666") up to be afflicted, and shall kill you: and ye shall be hated of all nations for my name's sake. And then shall many be offended, and shall betray one another, and shall hate one another. And many false prophets shall rise, and shall deceive many. And

because iniquity shall abound, the love of many shall wax cold. But he that shall endure unto the end, the same shall be saved [from death or thru death]. **And this gospel of the kingdom shall be preached** [by namely the 144,000 Jews & the 2 Witnesses] **in all the world for a witness unto all nations; and then shall the end come"** (Matt. 24:14).

The Church is now raptured, causing millions of Christians all over the globe to vanish or be "snatched away" from the earth. The RESULT will be worldwide chaos and confusion, as people try to explain the disappearance of millions from the earth. Planes flown by Christian pilots will no doubt crash to the earth. Streets, highways and tunnels will experience untold wreckage worldwide. Shipwrecks will even add to all the upheaval.

It's at this time when the Anti-Christ, **"that man of sin is revealed, the son of perdition; Who opposes and exalts himself above all that is called God or that is worshiped, so that he** [later during the Great Tribulation] **sits as God in the temple of God, showing himself that he is God"** (2 Thes. 2:3 b,4).

Profile of Anti-Christ

The Anti-Christ's personality will be both compelling and charismatic. He will be a brilliant orator, a political genius, and an economic guru; He will need no teller prompter and **have a mouth** (of eloquence) **speaking great things** [using pompous words](Dan. 7:8); He will be good looking (Dan. 7:20); He will be an undefeated military captain (Dan. 7:23); He will be shrewd and able to intrigue political adversaries (Dan. 11:21); He "most likely" will be a homosexual who is not interested in having children, and energized by Satan. Daniel 11:37 affirms, **"Neither shall he regard the God of his fathers, nor the desire of women, nor regard any god: for he shall magnify himself above all ".** When the Anti-Christ is revealed after the rapture (2 Thes. 2:1-7), he will quickly bring order and restoration to the worldwide calamity [resulting from the Rapture of the Church] and institute a "false peace".

SEVENTY WEEKS PROPHECY & PEACE TREATY WITH ISRAEL

Seventy weeks are determined upon thy people and upon the holy city, to finish the transgression, and to make an end of sins, and to make reconciliation for iniquity, and to bring in everlasting righteousness, and to seal up the vision and prophecy, and to anoint the most Holy. Know therefore and understand, that from the going forth of the commandment to restore and to build Jerusalem unto the Messiah the Prince (Anti-Christ) **shall be seven weeks** (of years), **and threescore and two weeks** (totaling 483 years)**: the street shall be built again, and the wall, even in troublous times. And after threescore and two weeks shall Messiah be cut off,** [which means that the crucifixion of Jesus will result in a gap of time] **but not for Himself: and the people of the prince that shall come shall destroy the city and the sanctuary; and the end thereof shall be with a flood, and unto the end of the war desolations are determined. And he** (Anti-Christ) **shall confirm the covenant with many for one week** (seven years)**: and in the midst** (middle) **of the week he shall cause the sacrifice and the oblation to cease, and for the overspreading of abominations he**

shall make it desolate, even until the consummation, and that determined shall be poured upon the desolate (Dan. 9:24-27).

Accordingly, the Anti-Christ will make a covenant with the Jews for a seven-year period, intending to provide peace for the nation of Israel. Nonetheless, during the Great Tribulation, the Anti-Christ will break this covenant and "**cause the sacrifice and the oblation to cease**". He will come and sit in the Temple [reserved for only Jesus Christ] and demand worship.

Gog & Magog

"**For nation shall rise against nation, and kingdom against kingdom.**" (Matt. 24:7). Among "nations rising against nations" will be the Gog & Magog invasion of Israel (Ezekiel 38,39). Here "Gog" refers to the anti-Christ, and "Magog" refers to his accompanying army. This battle will occur during Tribulation period, but prior to the battle at Armageddon (Rev. 16:16).

In the latter years, the nation of Israel shall dwell safely without walls (Ezek. 38: 8, 11). The armies of Russia, Germany, Persia, Ethiopia, Libya, etc. will all come against Israel (Ezek. 38: 5, 6). The fire of God's wrath will come with a massive earthquake, causing every man's sword to be against his brother (38:18-21). It will take 7 years to burn all the weaponry (39:9) and 7 months to bury the bones after every feathered fowl and every beast of the field have gathered to eat their flesh, and drink their blood (Ezek. 39:17). Scripture explains, **Alas! For that day is great, so that none is like it: it is the time of Jacob's trouble; but he shall be saved out of it** (Jer. 30:7), confirming God's faithfulness to Israel:

HISTORY OF ANTI-SEMITISM

From Isaac & Ishmael to Jacob & Esau, the family feud among the Jews and Arabs continue to the present day. Most Bible readers know the story: God promised the "childless" Abram that he would be a **father of many nations** (Gen. 17:5). And as often as Abram & Sarah may have tried, they could not have a child and it was [from their perspective] taking God took too long to deliver the promised child. So getting older and more impatient, Sarah suggested Abram hook up with her Egyptian maid Hagar. Abram complied and BAM: Hagar conceives and not only gets pregnant, but gets uppity. Sarah despises Hagar. Hagar eventually gets kicked out of the house. In her abandonment, the angel of the Lord visits Hagar and says to her, **"return to thy mistress, and submit thyself under her hands. And the angel of the Lord said unto her, I will multiply thy seed exceedingly, that it shall not be numbered for multitude. And the angel of the Lord said unto her, Behold , thou are with child, and shall bear a son, and shall call his name Ishmael; because the Lord hath heard thy affliction. And he will be a wild man; his hand will be against every man, and every man's hand against him; and he shall dwell in the presence of all his brethren** (Gen. 16:9-12).

Can you say, ISLAMIC TERRORISM? From these verses, we can clearly see why there will be no peace in the Middle East until the Prince of Peace (Isa. 9:6) sits on the throne in Jerusalem. SPECIAL THANKS to Abraham and Sarah who had to **lean to their own understanding** (Prov. 3:5). I say this facetiously. However, it is what it is. And the family feud continues to this very day.

Now Abram was 86 years old when Ishmael was born (Gen. 16:16). Thirteen years later, Abram has reached age 99, and his wife Sarah is 89. God steps back on the scene and promises Abram that he and Sarah will have Isaac "the promised child." the following year. Abram laughs (Gen. 17:17) and appeals for his firstborn Ismael to be "the promised child." GOD rejected Abraham's plea and chose Isaac instead in whom He would establish an everlasting covenant, but make Ishmael a great nation (Gen. 17:17-20).

In Genesis 25:33-34, the "firstborn" Esau **sold his birthright to Jacob** in exchange for bread and soup to satisfy his hunger, thereby **despising his birthright. So it is written, Jacob have I loved** (preferred), **but Esau I hated** (Romans 9:13).

Thus Psalm 83 reminds us of the continued generational sibling rivalry among the Jews and Arabs. In this passage, David prays, **"Keep not thou silence, O God: hold not thy peace, and be not still, O God. For, lo, thine enemies make a tumult: and they that hate thee have lifted up the head. They have taken crafty counsel against thy people** (the Israelites), **and consulted against thy hidden** (sheltered) **ones. They have said, Come, and let us cut them off from being a nation; that the name of Israel may be no more in remembrance. For they have consulted together with one consent** (heart): **they are confederate against thee. The tabernacles** (tents) **of Edom, and the Ishmaelites; of Moab, and the Hagarenes; Gebal, and Ammon, and Amelek; the Philistines with the inhabitants of Tyre fill their faces with shame; that they may seek thy name, O Lord. Let them be confounded and troubled forever; yea, let them be put to shame, and perish: That men may know** that thou, whose name is JEHOVAH, art the Most High over all the earth" (vss. 1-7, 16-18).

Scripture is very clear: GOD FIGHTS FOR ISRAEL (Josh. 10:42). **Thus says the Lord, which gives the sun for a light by day, and the ordinances of the moon and of the stars for a light by night, which divides the sea when the waves thereof roar; The Lord of hosts is His name: If those ordinances depart from before Me, says the Lord, then the seed of Israel also shall cease from being a nation before Me forever** (Jer. 31:35, 36). Please take a minute to ponder this truth: The nation of Israel is about the size of the state of New Jersey, and is surrounded by enemy nations whose consorted desire have always been to wipe Israel off the map. ISRAEL'S EXISTENCE IS CLEAR PROOF OF GOD'S EXISTENCE. No other nation has suffered more than Israel. And to mess with Israel is akin to poking GOD in the eye (Zech. 2:8).

Remember the call of Abram: **"Now the Lord had said unto Abram, Get thee out of thy country, and from thy kindred, and from thy father's house, unto a land that I will show thee. And I will make of thee a great nation, and I will bless thee, and make thy name great; and thou shalt be a blessing: And I will bless them** (namely the USA) **that bless thee, and curse him that curses thee: and in thee shall all families of the earth be blessed"** (Gen. 12:1-3). Hence the Jews of the flesh (well known for their ingenuity) are responsible for more inventions, innovations [including new technologies & advancements] than any other people.

According to GOD, there are only 2 people groups: Jews & Gentiles. And trust me; I know that some of you (God-haters who fume with anti-Semitism) may think that's so unfair. Here's my response: When you create your own universe, it (no doubt) would be your prerogative to identify more than 2 people groups. When that happens, we will gladly amalgamate and listen to you and your silly mandates. Until that happens, do yourself a BIG favor: **Humble yourselves therefore under the mighty hand of God, that He may exalt you in due time** (I Peter 5:6) when you resolve to stop fighting against, but BLESS ISRAEL.

2 Facts of Life

1) There is a GOD.

2) You are not HIM.

Fighting against GOD is FUTILE, to say the least . . . and eternally FATAL, to say the most:

And this is life eternal, that they might know thee the only true God, and Jesus Christ, whom thou hast sent (John 17:3).

5

WAR IN HEAVEN

Without question, Satan hates GOD.. and that's something he can do nothing about because GOD IS MATCHLESS. No creature can stand against his CREATOR. Satan's only option to counter GOD is a feeble attempt to destroy the very people GOD loves. Revelation 12 explains, **"And there appeared a great wonder in heaven; a woman** (Israel) **clothed with the sun** [depicting her as GOD's chosen nation], **and the moon under her feet** [alluding to GOD's promise of dominion], **and upon her head a crown of twelve stars** (representing the 12 tribes of Israel) Ref. Gen. 37:9)**: And she being with child** (Jesus Christ, the Messiah) **cried, travailing in birth, and pained to be delivered** [from the satanic attack of Jewish saints who will live on earth during the Great Tribulation period] (Rev. 12: 1,2).

THE GREAT RED DRAGON

And there appeared another wonder (sign) **in heaven; and behold a great red dragon, having seven heads and ten horns, and seven crowns upon his heads** (Rev. 12:3). The dragon is Satan himself. His red color reveals Satan's murderous character and desire to shed innocent blood (John 8:44; 10:10). His **seven heads** and **seven crowns** all reveal the completeness and worldwide influence of Satan's power. His **ten horns** refer to the fourth beast of Daniel 7 (vv. 7,24) and also connect with the Beast of the sea in Revelation 13, referring to the Anti-Christ. **And his tail drew the third part of the stars** (demons) **of heaven, and did cast them to the earth: and the dragon stood before the woman** (Mary) **which was ready to be delivered, for to devour her child** (Jesus) **as soon as it was born** (Rev. 12:4). "**And his tail drew the third part of the stars of heaven**" refers to Satan's original rebellion against GOD, causing him and his fallen angels to be kicked out of heaven onto the earth (cf. Is. 14:12-19; Ezek. 28:14-19). "**And the dragon stood before the woman** (Israel) **which was ready to be delivered, for to devour her child as soon as it was born**" referring to the birth of Christ.

In Matthew 2, we can read about the events surrounding the time of the birth of Jesus Christ. The totally insecure, mani-acal- king Herod would have no rivals to his throne. When wise men came from the east to Jerusalem to worship the new-born Christ, **Herod was troubled, and all Jerusalem with him** (vs. 3). Nonetheless, King Herod tells the wise men that he also would like to worship the child (vs. 8). A short time later, and after the wise men found and worshiped the child, and presented their gifts, Herod discovered that he was duped by the wise men whom **being warned of God in a dream that they should not return to Herod** (vs. 11-12). Herod, conse-quently goes BALLISTIC and into a murderous rage: **Then Herod, when he saw that he was mocked of the wise men, was exceeding wroth, and sent forth, and slew all the children that were in Bethlehem, and in all the coasts thereof, from** two years old and under, according to the time which he had diligently inquired of the wise men (v. 16).

Revelation 12:5 continues, **And she brought forth a man child, who was to rule all nations** (Ref. Psalm 2:7-9) **with a rod of iron: and her child** (Jesus) **was caught up unto God, and to His throne**.

In Acts 1:9-11, Jesus has returned to the earth after His resurrection. He reminded His disciples of the promise of the Holy Spirit (Ref. John 14:15-16) who will come to the earth and **dwell with them and be in them** shortly after His ascension to heaven. **And when He** (Jesus) **had spoken these things, while they beheld, He was taken up; and a cloud received Him out of their sight. And while they looked stedfastly toward heaven as He went up, behold two men stood by them in white apparel; Which also said, Ye men of Galilee, why stand ye gazing up into heaven? This same Jesus, which is taken up from you in to heaven, shall so come in like manner as ye have seen Him go into heaven.**

Revelation 12:6 continues, **And the woman** (Israel) **fled into the wilderness, where she hath a place prepared of God, that they should feed her there a thousand two hundred and three-score days.**

HERE THE 1,260 DAYS TRANSITIONS US FROM THE TRIBULATION PERIOD TO THE GREAT TRIBULATION PERIOD. At this time, Israel will take refuge among the Gentile nations where GOD will provide and protect her by using those Gentile believers who not only refused to receive "the mark" of the beast (Rev. 13;16), but also courageously aided many fugitives. These particular helpers will be acknowledged and rewarded when Jesus returns to the earth and judge the nations. They are identified as **the sheep on his right hand** (Matt. 25:33).

Now considering Revelation 12:7, it's important to note that events that happen in the natural world are precipitated by [and become a result] of events that have just occurred in the spirit world: **And there was a war in heaven: Michael and his angels fought against the dragon; and the dragon fought and his angels.** Please note: This will be a perfect match because all opponents will fight on their level. We know the expression all too well: "Pick on someone your own size." To put Iron Mike vs. Tiny Tim in the same ring, [we would all agree] be an unfair fight. Well, even more ridiculously absurd, would be putting any creature in the same ring with the CREATOR.

Remember these 3 statements of truth:

1) GOD HAS NO DIRECT OPPOSITE!!!

2) IT'S IMPOSSIBLE TO FIT OMNIPRESENCE in a ring.

3) GOD prepared HELL for the devil and his angels (Matt. 25:41).

The third truth I will elaborate further in chapter 12.

Continuing in verse 8, the dragon (Satan) and his angels **prevailed not; neither was their place found any more in heaven. And the great dragon was cast out, that old serpent, called the Devil, and Satan, which deceives the whole world: he was cast out into the earth, and his angels cast out with him. And I heard a loud voice saying in heaven, Now is come salvation, and strength, and the kingdom of our God, and the power of his Christ: for the accuser of our brethren is cast down, which accused them before our God day and night.**

At this time, Satan and his angels' access to heaven is permanently RESTRICTED. Because they all will be confined to the earth, scripture gravely warns, **Woe to the inhabitants of the earth and of the sea! For the devil is come down unto you, having great wrath, because he knows that he has but a short time. And when the dragon saw that he was cast unto the earth, he persecuted the woman** (Israel) **which brought forth the man child** (Jesus). **And to the woman were given two wings of a great eagle that she might fly into the wilderness** [which are the Gentile nations of the world], **into her place, where she is nourished for a time, and times, and half a time** [referring to the second 3 ½ years of the Great Tribulation period], **from the face of the serpent. And the serpent cast out of his mouth water as a flood after the woman** (Israel), **that he might cause her to be carried away of the flood** (of overwhelming evil and persecution) Rev. 12:9-15). These reactionary events mark the beginning of the Great Tribulation period on earth.

To be noted, Zechariah chapters 12-14 explicitly prophesy the future deliverance of Jerusalem and their relationship with the nations during the Great Tribulation and Millennium Periods. PLEASE READ, knowing that the devil (the enemy of our souls) will let us do anything, but read the Bible. Excuse me, again. I just had to throw that in parenthetically. No pressure here! You're doing fine reading up to this point. But PLEASE mark Zechariah chapters 12 – 14 on your calendar and in your planner because THE WORST INK IS BETTER THAN THE BEST MEMORY.

6

GREAT TRIBULATION
(Matt. 24:15-28)

When ye therefore shall see the ABOMINATION OF DESOLATION, spoken by Daniel the prophet, stand in the holy place, (whoever reads, let him understand:) Then let them which be in Judea flee into the mountains: Let him which is on the housetop not come down to take anything out of his house: And let him who is in the field not go back to take his clothes. But woe to those who are pregnant and to those who are nursing babies in those days! And pray that your flight may not be in winter or on the Sabbath.

And here are two reasons Jesus would warn all fugitives, trying to escape the tyranny of the Antichrist:

1) Being in any of these predicaments will expose hiding places and restrict travel.

2) The Sabbath will be the day of "enforced' worship of Satan's image (Rev. 13:15).

For then there will be great tribulation, such as has not been since the beginning of the world until this time, no, nor ever shall be. And unless those days were shortened, no flesh will be saved; but for the elect's sake those days will be shortened. Then if anyone says to you, Look, here is the Christ! or 'There' do not believe it. For false christs and false prophets will rise and show great signs and wonders to deceive, if possible, even the elect. See, I have told you beforehand. Therefore if they say to you, 'Look, He is in the desert!' do not go out; or 'Look, He is in the inner rooms!' do not believe it. For as the lightning comes from the east and flashes to the west, so also will the coming of the Son of Man be. For wherever the carcass is, there the eagles will be gathered together (Matt. 24:15-28). Here the "carcass" refers to all the dead bodies of armies worldwide who would come to battle against the **KING OF KINGS, AND LORD OF LORDS** (Rev. 19:16) who also will be accompanied with His bride, representing all the saints who were raptured and "snatched away" from the wrath to come, and dwell in heaven. Scripture confirms, **and the armies which were in heaven followed Him upon white horses, clothed in fine linen, white and clean** (Rev. 19:14).

Now I can hear someone saying fretfully, "But I'm afraid of horses." CALM DOWN! At this time, you will have a glorified "spiritual body" which means you will have the dual ability to ride on your horse or walk through it (1 Cor. 15:44, 2 Cor. 5:1). Falling off a horse will be impossible. Breaking your neck or suffering from any kind of physical injury will all be IMPOSSIBLE. Now let's go back to Rev. 12.

Again, the events in Revelation 12 will mark the beginning of the Great Tribulation period (second 3 ½ years) on earth. Continuing our reading with verse 16, **And the earth helped the woman** (Israel), **and the earth opened her mouth, and swallowed up the flood** (of overwhelming evil and persecution) **which the dragon cast out of his mouth. And the dragon was wroth with the woman** (Israel), **and went to make war with the remnant of her seed, which keep the commandments of God, and have the testimony of Jesus Christ** (vs. 17).

CAREER OF ANTICHRIST

Because Satan and the fallen angels are **"cast out into the earth"** (Rev. 12:9), and because Satan **knows that he has but a short time** (Rev. 12:12c) he commences his "temporary" 3 ½ years confinement on the earth with a BANG! In his consuming desire to be like GOD (Isaiah 14:14), he and the false trinity (the antichrist and false prophet) orchestrate a mock resurrection. What a DEBUT this will be for WORLDWIDE ACCLAIM!!!

In Revelation 13, the Antichrist is supposedly killed: **And the dragon** (Satan) **gave him** (the Antichrist) **his power, and his seat, and great authority. And I** (John) **saw one of his heads as it were wounded to death; and his deadly wound was healed: and all the world wondered after the beast** (the Antichrist). **And they worshiped the dragon which gave power unto the beast: and they worshiped the beast, saying, who is like unto the beast? Who is able to make war with him?** Feeling invincible, **and there was given unto him a mouth speaking great** (boisterous) **things and blasphemies; and power was given** unto him to continue forty and two months (3 ½ years). And he opened his mouth in blasphemy against God, to blaspheme His name, and His tabernacle, and them that dwell in heaven. And it was given unto him to make war with the saints, and to overcome them: and power was given unto him over all kindred, and tongues, and nations (to establish worldwide domination and a one world government). And all that dwell upon the earth shall worship him, whose names are not written in the book of life of the Lamb slain from the foundation of the world (Rev. 13:2b-8).

THE FALSE PROPHET

And I (John) beheld another beast [akin to the first, and having ecclesiastical authority], coming up out of the earth; he had two horns like a lamb (the impression of being gentle and harmless), and he spoke as a dragon. And he exercises all the power of the first beast before him (the Antichrist), and causes the earth and them which dwell therein to worship the first beast, whose deadly womb was healed. And he does great wonders (performing great signs) so that he even makes fire come down from heaven on the earth in the sight of men. And he deceives those who dwell on the earth by the means of those miracles which he had power to do in the sight of the beast; saying to them that dwell on the earth, that they should make an image to the beast, which had the wound by a sword, and did live. And he had power to give life (breath) unto the image of the beast, that the image of the beast should both speak, and cause as many as would not worship the image of the beast to be killed. He causes all, both small and great, rich and poor, free and slave, to receive a mark on their right hand or on their foreheads, and that no one may buy or sell, except the one who has the mark, or the name of the beast, or the number of his name. Here is wisdom. Let him that has understanding count the number of the beast; for it is the number of a man; and his number is 666 (Rev. 13:11-18). Because the Trinity [God the Father, God the Son, and God the Holy Ghost] made mankind on the sixth day (Gen. 1:31), the number 666 fitly describes mankind's divine makeup. Here we are reminded, **And God said , let Us make man in Our image, and according to Our likeness; let them have dominion over the fish of the sea, over the birds of the air, and over the cattle, over all the earth and over every creeping thing that creeps on the earth** (Gen. 1:26). AND PLEASE DON'T MISS THE TAIL END OF THE LAST VERSE. It's God's will that the saints rule over creeps, and not vice versa (cf. Ex. 18:21).

TATTOOS?

Some speculate whether the number 666 will be an embedded chip or an obvious tattoo. I believe perhaps both: a biochip to institute a cashless payment system to electronically transfer payments, and "the mark" to be readily recognized, showing allegiance to the Anti-Christ, in order to "buy or sell."

Today, tattoo businesses flourish and are patronized by both Christians and sinners alike. No doubt most individuals who have tattoos are often influenced by peer pressure, professional athletes or celebrity elites. However, to all the CARNAL Christians who must think and act like the world, you can take this observation for whatever it is worth: At age 56, I've never seen an occupied home or church building plastered with graffiti. When Jesus said in Matt. 16:18, **"I will build my church"**, he was not referring to a brick and mortar building. **"My church"** is synonymous with **"My people."** Scripture is clear: **Ye also, as lively stones, are built up a spiritual house, a holy priesthood, to offer up spiritual sacrifices, acceptable to God by Jesus Christ** (1 Peter 2:5). If plastering the physical house of any worship building with graffiti is unacceptable, what makes you think GOD is pleased when you desecrate the natural body with (so-called) body art? Regarding fornication and even tattoos, Scripture begs the question: **What? Know ye not that your body is the temple of the Holy Ghost which is in you, which ye have of God, and ye are not your own? For ye are bought with a price: therefore glorify God in your body, and in your spirit, which are God's** (1 Cor. 6:19,20).

Whenever CARNAL Christians decide to tattoo their bodies, they operate in defiance to Leviticus 19:28: **You shall not make any cuttings in your flesh for the dead, nor tattoo any marks on you: I am the Lord.** It's quite interesting how some carnal Christians will even try to placate GOD with a Bible verse tattooed on their skin. Saints, please remember that GOD's Word is to be **hidden in our hearts** (Ps. 119:11), and not painted on our skin. Your carnal thinking will only continue the wasted time and money playing on the Devil's playground. And he smiles every time he sees you visit the tattoo parlor. Hopefully, one day you will grow up and realize the folly of your ways. If not, just be assured that you will NEVER lose your "fire insurance."

During the Millennium and the Eternal State, our "glorified" spiritual bodies will be tattoo-free. And if that prospect is so daunting and disappointing to some of you, it's time to **"examine yourselves, whether you be in the faith; prove your own selves, how that Jesus Christ is in you, except you be reprobates? But I trust you that we are not reprobates"** (2 Cor. 13:5, 6). To know better is to do better. NO MORE TATTOOS for the Christians and the Jews!

I didn't say it. GOD SAID IT!!!

Nonetheless, during the Great Tribulation, people will readily accept having a tattoo **"on their right hand or on their foreheads"** (Rev. 13:16) in order to participate in the marketplace for survival. At this time, herd conformity to any government mandate or edict will be commonplace, seeing that all the "crazy" Christians have vanished from the earth, and took "law and order" with them.

ARE YOU GETTING IT? There's no one left behind to **contend for the faith** (Jude 3). The Bible aptly explains: **They that forsake the law praise the wicked: but such as keep the law contends with them** (Prov. 28:4). And at this time, the world's contenders have been raptured or mostly killed, and dwell in heaven: **And I saw thrones, and they sat upon them, and judgment was given unto them: and I saw the souls of them that were beheaded for the witness of Jesus, and for the word of God, and which had not worshiped the beast, neither his image, neither had received his mark upon their foreheads, or in their hands; and they lived and reigned with Christ a thousand years** (Rev. 20:4).

GOD's Wrath & Satan's Fury

GOD's wrath will be reflected in the **SEAL** judgments, the **TRUMPET** judgments, and the **BOWL** judgments. Robert Jeffress' book, PERFECT ENDING, sums it best on pages 111-115.:

1. The Seal Judgments

"The seal judgments, described in Revelation 6, began with the rise of Antichrist (6:1-2), and include war (6:3-4), famine (6:5-6), death from the famine that will destroy one-fourth of the world's population (6:7-8), martyrdom of those converted after the Rapture of the Church (6:9-11), and tremendous cosmological disturbances (6:12-17). The final seal judgment actually contains all of the trumpet judgments described in Revelation 8:2-11:5."

2. The Trumpet Judgments

"The trumpet judgments (described in Revelation 8-9), are directed against nature. During the first trumpet judgment, God uses a mixture of hail and fire to destroy one-third of the earth's vegetation. The second trumpet judgment involves 'something like a great mountain burning with fire' falling into the sea (Revelation 8:8) which could be a giant asteroid. Asteroids are chunks of rocks ranging from a few feet long to several miles in diameter. This judgment will destroy one-third of all marine life and one-third of all the ships, resulting in ecological and economic disaster.

A falling star will destroy one third of the earth's freshwater supply during the third trumpet judgment (8:10-11). The fourth trumpet judgment will involve a disruption of the rotation pattern of the earth and moon, causing wide fluctuations in temperature (8:12).

During the fifth trumpet judgment, described in Revelation 9:11-12, Satan (the "star from heaven") unleashes demonic tormentors to persecute mankind, except those who have been sealed by God. These torturers are described as locusts with a sting comparable to scorpions; but their power is derived from Satan [as was previously discussed under the topic, **Hell on Earth**].

The sixth trumpet judgment involves the assembling of a massive army of two million soldiers (Revelation 9:16) who are later described as coming from the east (Revelation 16:12-16). We should probably understand this army as a human army that demonically empowered by four demons (described as "angels" in Revelation 9:15). The battle described beginning in Revelation 9:18 may be the beginning of the war we refer to as Armageddon, which could extend for several years until the return of Christ. John noted that this war kills one third of mankind (Revelation 9:18). When you combine this number with those already killed as a result of the fourth seal judgment (one-fourth of the earth according to Revelation 6:8), it means that one-half of the world's population has been destroyed. Now we can see why Jesus said that unless these days had been cut short, no one would have survived."

3. The Bowl Judgments

The bowl judgments are described in Revelation 16:1-21. "But while the trumpet judgments affected only a portion of the earth, these judgments impact the entire planet. The rapidity of these judgments probably occurs over the span of just a few days and leads up to the return of Jesus Christ. The final bowl judgment is especially severe:

Then the seventh angel poured out his bowl upon the air, and a loud voice came out of the temple from the throne, saying, "It is done." And there were flashes of lightning and sounds and peals of thunder; and there was a great earthquake, such as there had not been since man came to be upon the earth, so great an earthquake was it, and so mighty. The great city was split into three parts, and the cities of the nations fell. Babylon the great was remembered before God, to give her the cup of the wine of His fierce wrath (Rev. 16:17-19).

Since this judgment is poured out 'upon the air' and is accompanied by 'flashes of lightning' and 'peals of thunder,' some have speculated that John is describing a nuclear explosion. If so, it results in a destruction of Babylon—most likely to reference to whatever city is the seat of the Antichrist's power."(pages 111-115).

Satan's Fury can be summarized in Daniel 7:25. **And he** (the Antichrist) **shall speak great** (pompous) **words against the most High, and shall wear out** (persecute and afflict) **the saints of the most High, and think to change times and laws** (whether of Divine or human authority) into a general spirit of lawlessness and unbelief): **and they shall be given into his hand until a time and times and the dividing of time** (3 ½ years or 1,260 days or 42 months)."Reference Daniel 12:7, Revelation 11:2; 12:6, 14; 13:5.

Incidentally, THE BIBLE WILL NOT BE THE #1 BESTSELLER BOOK DURING THIS TIME because the Antichrist and his goons will control all information. With the supreme God-hater in charge, most Bibles and Christian materials will all be banned, confiscated and burned. Without the Bible, it will be most difficult to become a Christian during this time because **"Faith comes by hearing, and hearing by the word of God"** (Rom. 10:17).

7

ARMAGEDDON & THE RESTRUCTURED EARTH
(Rev. 16:12-21)

And the sixth angel poured out his vial upon the great river Euphrates where I believe the 200 million demons were bound near it, and all were released (9:14)**; and the water thereof dried up** due to the extreme heat from the sun in the fourth bowl judgment (vss. 8, 9), **that the way of the kings of the east** (China, India and other Oriental nations) **might be prepared** to reach their ultimate destination which is "Armageddon" in the land of Palestine. However, unknown to the soldiers, it's a DIVINE TRAP!

Remember when GOD parted the Red Sea, it led to the destruction of the Egyptian army (Exodus 14:21). Here drying up the river Euphrates will allow the kings of the east and their armies to reach the ultimate destination to their destruction— that being, the Battle of Armageddon in the land of Palestine. **And I saw three unclean spirits** (demons) **like frogs come out of the mouth of the dragon, and out of the mouth of the false**

prophet. For they are the spirits of devils, working miracles, which go forth unto the kings of the earth and of the whole world, to gather them to the battle to fight against the second coming of Christ (cf. 19:19), which also referenced as, **of that great day of God Almighty.**

Please note: It is GOD who commissions the demons, and not Satan. Satan is GOD's devil who will remain on GOD's leash until he is cast into the lake of fire (Rev. 20:10). Consider a related episode where GOD used lying spirits to accomplish His will on the earth:

In 1 Kings 22, King Ahab is seduced by false prophets. **"And the king of Israel said unto Jehoshaphat, Did I not tell thee that he would prophesy no good concerning me, but evil? And he said, Hear thou therefore the word of the Lord: I saw the Lord sitting on His throne, and all the host of heaven** (Job 1:6; 2:1) **standing by Him on His right hand and on His left. And the Lord said unto Him, Wherewith? And He said, I will go forth, and I will be a lying spirit in the mouth of all his prophets. And he said, Thou shalt persuade him, and prevail also: go forth, and do so. Now therefore, behold, the Lord hath put a lying spirit in the mouth of all these thy prophets, and the Lord hath spoken evil concerning thee** (18-23).

Thus the kings and their armies (worldwide) will all believe that their motivation is one of self-will, rather than the influence of lying spirits. This same deception will ultimately lead to their demise. As Proverbs 8:36 aptly puts it: **But he who sins against me wrongs his own soul: all those who hate me love death.** And GOD (in His sovereignty) will release a lying spirit to order every enemy's behavior to carry out the fulfillment of their own demise.

During this climactic time, Jesus admonishes the believers: **For false Christs and false prophets shall rise, and shall show signs and wonders, to seduce, if it were possible, even the elect** (Mark 13:22).

In Joel 3:1-2, this same event is prophesied: **For behold in those days, and in that time, when I (GOD) shall bring against the captivity of Judah and Jerusalem. I will gather all nations, and will bring them down into the valley of Jehoshaphat, and will plead with them there for my people and for my heritage Israel, whom they have scattered among the nations, and parted my land.. Assemble yourselves, and come, all ye heathen** (nations), **and gather yourselves together round about: thither cause thy mighty ones to come down, O Lord** (vs. 11). **Let the heathen be wakened, and come up to the valley of Jehoshaphat: for there will I sit to judge all the nations around about** (vs. 12). **Put ye in the sickle** (cf. Rev. 14:14), **for the harvest is ripe: come, get you down; for the press is full, the vats overflow; for their wickedness is great. Multitudes, multitudes in the valley of decision: for the day of the Lord is near in the valley of decision** (vss. 13-14) (referencing Armageddon). ARE YOU STILL PAYING ATTENTION? Do you need another water break? Take your time! We'll wait for you. Now let's continue.

Please observe that the companion passage for Joel 3 is Revelation 14:14-20 which is a reference to the coming Battle of Armageddon (Rev. 16:14-16). And to speak of GORY details, the amount of human blood spilled from this war, will become a great flood of blood that will so boggle the mind. Revelation 14:20 reports: **And the winepress was trodden** (trampled) **without** (outside) **the city** (of Jerusalem)**, and blood came out of the winepress, even unto the horse bridles** (which is about four feet), **by the space of a thousand and six hundred furlongs** (which is approximately 184 miles, the full length of Palestine). Again, to the "Rough & Tough" recalcitrant, we are soberly reminded: **It is a fearful thing to fall into the hands of the living God** (Heb. 10:31).

Continuing in Joel 3:15, **the sun and the moon shall be darkened, and the stars shall withdraw their shining. The Lord shall roar out of Zion, and utter His voice from Jerusalem, and the heavens and the earth shall shake** (cf. Rev. 16:18): **But the Lord will be the hope of His people, and the strength of the children of Israel** (Joel 3:1, 2, 11-16).

Continuing in Revelation. 16:15: **Behold, I** (Jesus) **come as a thief. Blessed is he that watches, and keeps his garments,** [an exhortation to the surviving believers] **lest he walks naked, and they see his shame. And He gathered them together into a place called in the Hebrew tongue Armageddon. And the seventh angel poured out his vial** (alluding to the destruction of the great city Babylon) **into the air; and there came a great voice out of the temple of heaven, from the throne, saying, IT IS DONE** (signifying that with this vial and the return of Christ Himself, the judgments are now finished). **And there were voices, and thunders, and lightnings; and there was a great earthquake, such as was not since men were upon the earth, so mighty an earthquake, and so great. And the great** city (16:19) was divided into three parts, and the city of the nations fell: and great Babylon came in remembrance before God, to give unto her the cup of the wine of the fierceness of His wrath. And every island fled away, and the mountains were not found. And there fell upon men a great hail out of heaven, every stone about the weight of a talent (60 – 100 pounds): and men blasphemed God because of the plague of the hail; for the plague thereof was exceeding great.

8

THE FALL OF BABYLON /
God Judges The World System
(Rev. 17, 18)

And there came one of the seven angels which had seven vials, and talked with me (John), saying unto me, Come hither, I will show unto thee the judgment of the great whore (Ref. Nahum 3:4) who sits upon many waters (17: 15). With whom the kings of the earth have committed fornication (spiritual infidelity) and the inhabitants of the earth have been made drunk with the wine of her fornication (18:3). So he carried me away in the spirit into the wilderness: and I saw a woman (Babylon The Great Prostitute) sit upon a scarlet-colored beast (the first century city of Rome), full of names of blasphemy [the religious system's utter disdain for GOD], having seven heads and ten horns (identified in verses 9, 10 and 12). And the woman was arrayed in purple and scarlet color, and decked with gold and precious stones and pearls [showing her wealth and attraction], having a golden cup in her hand full of abominations and filthiness of her fornication [referring to her apostasy and activities that are filthy and abominable to GOD]. **And upon her forehead was a name written, MYSTERY, BABYLON THE GREAT, THE MOTHER OF HARLOTS AND ABOMINATIONS OF THE EARTH.**

Here "the ancient Babylon prefigures this future Babylon. The harlot will do what literal Babylon did in the past: (1) oppress God's people, and (2) propagate a false religious system. Much of the world's idolatry can be traced back to historical Babylon (cf. Gen. 11:1-9). This harlot has killed many of God's saints and Christian martyrs throughout the ages, and will do so again during the Tribulation period" (The King James Study Bible, Copyright 1988, page 2007).

And I saw the woman drunken with the blood of the saints, and with the blood of the martyrs of Jesus: and when I saw her, I wondered with great admiration. And the angel said unto me, Wherefore did thou marvel? I will tell thee the mystery of the woman, and of the beast that carried her, which had the seven heads and ten horns. The beast that thou saw was [It existed in the form of the ancient Roman Empire] **, and is not** [It has not existed as an empire since the fifth century and will not exist again until the Antichrist gains worldwide authority during the Tribulation period]; **and shall ascend out of the bottomless pit** [Satan will raise up the Antichrist as his false messiah and give him worldwide rule (cf. 11:7; 13:3,4)], **and go into perdition** [the lake of fire (cf. 19:20)]: **and they that dwell on the earth shall wonder, whose names were not written in the book of life from the foundation of the world, when they behold the beast that was, and is not, and yet is. And here is the mind which hath wisdom. The seven heads are seven**

mountains, on which the woman sits. And there are seven kings [who may represent seven rulers in the Roman Empire]: **five are fallen** (are past), **and one is** [referring to the Roman Empire existing at the time of John], **and the other is not yet come** [alluding to the revived Roman Empire in Daniel by the 10 toes in the image of Daniel 2:41-44 and by the 10 horns on the fourth beast of Daniel 7:7, 20,24 and in Revelation by the 10 horns on the first Beast (13:1; 17:3, 12,13)], **and when he comes, he must continue a short space. And the beast** (Antichrist) **that was, and is not, even he is the eighth, and is of the seven** [culmination of all the previous, pagan, idolatrous empires], **and goes into perdition** [which is the lake of fire – v. 8; 19:20]. **And the ten horns which thou saw are ten kings, which have received no kingdom as yet; but receive power as kings one hour with the beast. These have one mind, and shall give their power** (political authority) **and strength** (military power) **unto the beast** [to conquer the earth]. **These shall make war with the Lamb, and the Lamb shall overcome them: for He is the Lord of lords, and King of kings: and they that are with Him are called, and chosen, and faithful. And He said unto me, the waters which thou saw, where the whore sits, are peoples, and multitudes, and nations, and tongues** [representing the populated world]. **And the ten horns which thou saw upon the beast, these shall hate the whore** [the apostate church which is the world religion headed by the false prophet] **and shall make her desolate and naked, and shall eat her flesh, and burn her with fire. For God hath put in their hearts to fulfill His will, and to agree, and give their kingdom unto the beast, until the words of God shall be fulfilled. And the woman which thou saw is that great city, which reigns over the kings of the earth.**

Please remember: Because the devil and his fallen angels were defeated and kicked out of heaven by Michael and his angels, they are now temporarily confined to the earth (Rev. 12:7-9). Hence the devil, in his preoccupation to be like GOD (Isaiah 14:14), will finally have his moment. As time quickly wanes, Satan will no longer tolerate competition with the world religion, headed by the False Prophet. Thus GOD will use him as a puppet to destroy it. John MacArthur explains:

"Antichrist's self-serving, satanically inspired actions are, however, precisely in the scope of God's sovereign plan. In fact, it is **God** who will **put it in** the **hearts** of Antichrist's followers **to execute His purpose by having a common purpose, and by giving their kingdom to the beast.** God's power is behind the destruction and consolidation of the evil empire; as always, Satan is the instrument of God's purposes. The one-world unification government so long sought by the humanists will have finally arrived, only to be destroyed in one great act of divine judgment. All **the words of God**—every prophecy of Christ's return and the setting up of His kingdom—**will be fulfilled** completely" (The MacArthur New Testament Commentary, Revelation 12-22, page 172).

Revelation chapter 18 continues: **And after these things I saw another angel come down from heaven, having great power; and the earth was lightened** (illuminated) **with His glory. And he cried mightily with a strong voice, saying, Babylon the great is fallen, is fallen, and is become the habitation of devils, and the hold of every foul spirit, and a cage of every unclean and hateful bird.** Again, this aftermath is the direct result of Satan and the fallen angels' being cast out into the earth (12:9).

Their swift destructive activities (all the more) confirm John 10:10, **"The thief comes not, but for to steal, and to kill, and to destroy. I** (Jesus) **am come that they might have life, and that they may have it more abundantly."**

For all nations have drunk of the wine of the wrath of her for-nication (spiritual apostasy)**, and the kings of the earth have committed fornication with her, and the merchants of the earth are waxed rich through the abundance of her delica-cies** (luxuries)**. And I heard another voice from heaven, saying, Come out of her, my people** (tribulation saints and fugitives who refuse to take the mark 666)**, that ye be not partakers of her sins, and that ye receive not her plagues. For her sins have reached unto heaven, and God hath remembered her iniqui-ties. Reward her even as she rewarded you, and double unto her double according to her works: in the cup which she hath filled fill to her double.** It's now JUDGMENT TIME! 'Pay Day, Some Day' has become That AWLFUL Day.

Interestingly, the Babylonian system began in Genesis 10, and has continued to the present day. Even the prophets gave warn-ings to flee ancient Babylon: Isa. 48:20; Jer. 50:8, 51:6, 45; Zech. 2;6-7. Believers today are also admonished to **be not conformed to the world system, but be transformed by the renewing of your mind, that you may prove what is that good, and accept-able, and perfect will of God** (Rom. 12:2).

Continuing in Revelation 18: 7, **How much she hath glorified herself, and lived luxuriously, so much torment and sorrow give her: for she said in her heart, I sit a queen** [proud and arrogant]**, and am no widow** [self-confident, lacking nothing]**,**

and shall see no sorrow [feeling impregnable and invincible]. **Therefore shall her plagues come** [suddenly] **in one day, death, and mourning, and famine; and she shall be utterly burned with fire: for strong is the Lord God who judges her. And the kings of the earth, who have committed fornication and lived luxuriously with her, shall bewail her, when they shall see the smoke of her burning, Standing afar off for the fear of her torment, saying, Alas, alas, that great city Babylon, that mighty city! For in one hour is thy judgment come.** Satan's [the god of this world] last and greatest worldwide pagan economic system has now collapsed. **And the merchants of the earth shall weep and mourn over her; for no man buys their merchandise any more. The merchandise of gold, and silver, and precious stones, and of pearls, and fine linen, and all thyine wood, and all manner vessels of ivory, and all manner vessels of most precious wood, and of brass, and iron, and marble. And cinnamon, and odors, and ointments, and frankincense, and wine, and oil, and fine flour, and wheat, and beasts, and sheep, and horses, and chariots, and slaves, and souls of men.**

INTERPRETATION: All stock indices in every market sector will plummet to zero, causing everyone to lose their entire investment. **And the fruits** (of luxury and splendor) **that thy soul lusted after are departed from thee, and all things which were dainty and goodly** [referring to show-off pieces and good luck charms] **are departed from thee, and thou shalt find them no more at all** [because there will be NO MORE ONLINE OR IN-PERSON SHOPPING in that all commerce has ended]. **The merchants of these things which were made rich by her, shall stand afar off for the fear of her torment, weeping and wailing, And saying, Alas, alas, that great** city, that was clothed in fine linen, and purple, and scarlet, and decked with gold, and precious stones, and pearls! For in one hour so great riches is come to nought (nothing). And every shipmaster, and all the company in ships (cruise lines), and sailors, and as many as trade by sea, stood afar off, And cried when they saw the smoke of her burning, saying, what city is like unto this great city! And they cast dust on their heads, and cried, weeping and wailing, saying, Alas, alas, that great city, wherein were made rich all that had ships in the sea by reason of her wealth! For in one hour is she made desolate. Rejoice over her, thou heaven, and ye holy apostles and prophets: for God hath avenged you on her. And a mighty angel took a stone like a great millstone, and cast it into the sea, saying, Thus with violence shall that great city Babylon be thrown down, and shall be found no more at all [NO MORE RECOVERY]. And the voice of the harpers, and musicians, and of pipers, and trumpeters, shall be heard no more at all in thee [NO MORE ENTERTAINMENT]; and no craftsman, of whatsoever craft he be, shall be found any more in thee [NO MORE INDUSTRIES]; and the sound of a millstone shall be heard no more at all in thee [NO MORE RESTAURANTS] (vs. 8); And the light of the candle shall shine no more at all in thee [NO MORE ELECTRICITY, causing TOTAL BLACKOUT]; and the voice of the bridegroom and of the bride shall be heard no more at all in thee [NO MORE WEDDINGS]: for thy merchants were the great men of the earth; for by thy sorceries [of witchcraft, palm reading, tarot cards, transcendental meditation, illegal drug use, necromancy . . . Ref. Deut. 18:9-12] were all nations deceived. And in her was found the blood of prophets, and of saints, and of all that were slain upon the earth.

In conclusion, we can clearly see that after the Antichrist was able to build the greatest commercial empire the world has ever known, GOD will totally destroy it for three reasons: 1) its arrogance, 2) its worldwide apostasy, and 3) its persecution and martyrdom of GOD's people.

9

WORLD WAR III
(Rev.19:11-21; 20:1-3)

And I saw heaven opened, and behold a white horse; and He (Jesus) **that sat upon him was called Faithful and True, and in righteousness He will judge and make war** [as He returns to the earth in victorious conquest]. **His eyes were as a flame of fire** (sharper and more piercing than any X-ray vision), **and on His head were many crowns** [to indicate total sovereignty and authority]; **and He had a name written, that no man knew, but He Himself** (being the ONLY OMNISISCIENT ONE). **And He was clothed with a vesture dipped in** (the) **blood** (of His enemies) (cf. Isa. 63:1): **and His name is called The Word of God** (which presents Jesus Christ as the revelation of GOD (cf. John 1:1, 14, 18, John 10:30, John 14:9, 1 John 1:1-3), **And the armies** [including the saints of all ages: Old Testament Saints, New Testament Saints, Church Age Saints, Tribulation Saints, and Martyred Saints] **which were in heaven followed Him upon white horses, clothed in fine linen, white and clean. And out of His mouth goes a sharp sword** (Rev. 1:16; Eph. 4:12**), that with it He should smite the nations**

(Isaiah 11:4): **and He shall rule them with a rod of iron** [sig-
nifying that Christ will subject all nations to Himself during
the Millennium Period (20:4)]: **And He treads the winepress
of the fierceness and wrath of Almighty God** (vs. 15). **And He
hath on His vesture and on His thigh a name written, KING
OF KINGS, AND LORD OF LORDS** (vs. 16).

Please note how Rev. 19:16 connects to Rev. 17:14: **These** (coa-
lition of kings, along with the Antichrist and False Prophet)
**shall make war with the Lamb, and the Lamb shall overcome
them: for He is Lord of lords, and King of kings: and they** (His
armies) **that are with Him are called, and chosen, and faithful.**
These two verses both refer to the battle of Armageddon in
Rev. 16:16. The reason I refer to this battle as World War III
is because scripture clearly explains in Rev. 16:14, **For they are
the spirits of devils, working miracles, which go forth unto
the kings of the earth and of the whole world, to gather them
to the battle of that great day of God Almighty.**

In Rev. 19:17, we read, **And I** (John) **saw an angel standing
in the sun; and he cried with a loud voice, saying to all the
fowls** (vultures) **that fly in the midst of heaven, Come and
gather yourselves together unto the supper of the great God.**
[This is NOT the marriage supper of the Lamb that takes place
in heaven] (vs. 9); **That ye may eat the flesh of captains, and
the flesh of mighty men, and the flesh of horses, and of them
that sit on them, and the flesh of all men, both free and bond,
both small and great** (vs. 18). Here GOD calls all the birds
and vultures of the sky to **gather** and **eat the flesh** of all men
and animals that have died in the Battle of Armageddon (Rev.
16:14,16). Verse 19 continues, **And I saw the beast** (Antichrist)

and the kings of the earth, and their armies, gathered together to make war against Him that sat on the horse, and against His army. Here the armies of the Antichrist coupled with the armies of the kings of all the earth, will gather in Palestine at Armageddon (cf. 16;12-16) to attempt to prevent the second return and kingdom of Jesus Christ.

And the beast was taken, and with him the false prophet that wrought miracles before him, with which he deceived them that had received the mark of the beast, and them that worshiped his image. REALLY? Where are the fireworks? We expect to read about swords drawn, bullets flying, and missiles released. But before there's any provocation, the battle is "point blank" over.

WHAT A MIGHTY GOD WE SERVE! Jesus speaks a word, and the whole war is over. In an instant, **these both** (the Antichrist and false prophet) **were cast alive into a lake of fire burning with brimstone** (vs. 20). **And the remnant were slain with the sword of Him that sat upon the horse, which sword proceeded out of His mouth:**

Just remember that we serve a speaking GOD who spoke everything into existence, including angels, galaxies, gnats . . . all things visible and invisible. **For by Him all things were created that are in heaven and that are on earth, visible and invisible, whether thrones or dominions or principalities or powers. All things were created through Him and for Him** (Col. 1:16). And how did GOD do it? By His Word: **By the word of the LORD were the heavens made; and all the host of them by the breath of His mouth** (Ps. 33:6). Continuing in verse 21, **and all the fowls were filled with their flesh** (referring to the bodies of those who died in the Battle of Armageddon).

The prophet Zechariah cites a few details of this climatic event:

Behold the day of the Lord is coming, and thy spoil shall be divided in the midst of thee. For I will gather all nations against Jerusalem to battle; and the city shall be taken, and he houses rifled (plundered), **and the women ravished; and half of the city shall go forth unto captivity, and the residue** (remnant) **of the people shall not be cut off from the city. Then shall the Lord go forth into captivity, and fight against those nations as when He fought in the day of battle. And His feet shall stand in that day upon the mount of Olives, which is before Jerusalem on the east, and the mount of Olives shall cleave** (split) **in the midst thereof toward the east and toward the west, and there shall be a very great valley; and half of the mountain shall move toward the north, and half of it toward the south. And you shall flee to the valley of the mountains; for the valley of the mountains shall reach unto Azal: Yes, you shall flee as you fled from the earthquake in the days of Uzziah king of Judah. Thus the Lord my God will come, and all the saints with you. It shall come to pass in that day that there will be no light; The lights will diminish. It shall be one day which is known to the Lord—Neither day nor night. But at evening time it shall happen that it will be light. And in that day it shall be that living waters shall flow from Jerusalem; half of them toward the eastern sea and half of them toward the western sea; In both summer and winter it shall occur. And the Lord shall be king over all the earth. In that day it shall be one LORD, and His name ONE. And the land**

shall be turned as a plain from Geba to Rimmon south of Jerusalem: and it shall be lifted up, and inhabited in her place, from Benjamin's gate unto the place of the first gate, unto the corner gate, and from the tower of Hananeel unto the king's winepresses. And men shall dwell in it, and there shall be no more utter destruction; but Jerusalem shall be safely inhabited. And this shall be the plague wherewith the Lord will smite all the people that have fought against Jerusalem; Their flesh shall consume away in their holes (sockets), and their tongue shall consume away in their mouth. And it shall come to pass in that day, that a great tumult from the Lord shall be among them; and they shall lay hold everyone on the hand of his neighbor, and his hand shall rise up against the hand of his neighbor. And Judah also shall fight at Jerusalem; and the wealth of all the heathen round about shall be gathered together, gold, and silver, and apparel, in great abundance. And it shall come to pass, that every one that is left of all the nations which came against Jerusalem shall even go up from year to year [during the Millennium]to worship the King, the LORD of hosts, and to keep the feast of tabernacles (Zech. 14:1-14,16)

Now if the largest human battle in world history is over before it starts, and if you have any trouble grasping that truth, here's A REALITY CHECK: Just imagine creating something, and the very thing you created seeks to defeat, destroy and dethrone you. Now you can see why GOD laughs at the wicked (Ps. 37:13).

Scripture sums it up this way: **For evildoers shall be cut off: but those that wait upon the Lord, they shall inherit the earth. For yet a little while, and the wicked shall not be: yea thou** shalt diligently consider (look for) his place, and it shall not be. But the meek shall inherit the earth; and shall delight themselves in the abundance of peace. The wicked plotted against the just, and gnashes upon him with his teeth. The Lord shall laugh at him: for He sees that his day is coming. The wicked have drawn out the sword, and have bent their bow, to cast down the poor and needy, and to slay such as be of upright conversation (conduct). Their sword shall enter into their own heart, and their bows shall be broken. A little that a righteous man hath is better than the riches of many wicked. For the arms of the wicked shall be broken: but the Lord upholds the righteous. The Lord knows the days of the upright: and their inheritance shall be forever. They shall not be ashamed in the evil time: and in the days of famine they shall be satisfied. But the wicked shall perish, and the enemies of the Lord shall be as the fat of lambs [enjoyed by the birds of the sky]: they shall consume (vanish); into smoke [of hell fire and everlasting torment] they consume away [eternally and without escape] (Ps. 37:9-20).

And I saw an angel come down from heaven, having the key of the bottomless pit, and a great chain in his hand. And he laid hold on the dragon, that old serpent, which is the Devil, and Satan, and bound him a thousand years, And cast him into the bottomless pit, and shut him up, and set a seal upon him [and not the pit], that he should deceive the nations no more, till the thousand years should be fulfilled: and after that he must be loosed a little season.

10

JUDGMENT OF NATIONS
(Matt. 25:31-46, 24:40, 41)

Now that (Armageddon) the greatest battle in world history is over in an instant, we now come to the judgment of nations. Keep in mind, citizens don't go to war, but do become subjects of the new ruling authorities.

When the Son of man shall come in His glory, and all the holy angels with Him, then shall He sit upon the throne of His glory: And before Him shall be gathered all nations (of people who survived the Great Tribulation): **and He** (Jesus Christ) **shall separate them one from another, as a shepherd divides his sheep from the goats: And He shall set the sheep on His right hand, but the goats on the left. Then shall the King say unto them on His right hand, Come, ye blessed of my Father; inherit the kingdom prepared for you from the foundation of the world: For I was an hungered, and ye gave Me meat** [referencing the starving fugitives who refused the mark 666 during the Great Tribulation]: **I was thirsty, and ye gave Me drink: I was a stranger, and ye took Me in: Naked,**

and ye clothed Me: I was sick, and ye visited Me: I was in prison, and ye came unto Me. Then shall the righteous answer Him, saying, Lord, when saw we thee an hungered, and fed thee? Or thirsty, and gave thee drink? When saw we thee a stranger, and took thee in? or naked, and clothed thee? Or when saw we thee sick, or in prison, and came unto thee? And the King shall answer and say unto them, Verily I say unto you, Inasmuch as ye have done it unto one of the least of these my brethren [especially during the Great Tribulation], ye have done it unto Me.

Then shall He say also unto them on the left hand [who received the mark 666], Depart from me, ye cursed, into everlasting fire, prepared for the devil and his angels (vs. 41):

Please note: When GOD made hell, it was not a place for humankind. He prepared HELL for the devil and his angels. However, if you reject Jesus Christ as your personal Lord & Savior, GOD will respect your choice. I repeat, GOD DOES NOT SEND ANYONE TO HEAVEN. GOD DOES NOT SEND ANYONE TO HELL. WE CHOOSE. AND GOD RESPECTS OUR CHOICE. It's interesting how the Satanists, occults, sorcerers, witches, palm readers, godless astrologers, and evil people in general, -- not overlooking the erudite and intellectuals who are too smart to need a Savior --these have mostly concluded that if there is a hell, they will receive brownie points and get favor badges from the devil when they arrive . . . not knowing that HELL is the last place the devil and his angels would want to enter and experience: And the devil that deceived them was cast into the lake of fire and brimstone, where the beast (Antichrist) and false prophet are, and shall

be tormented day and night forever and ever (Rev. 20:10). At that time, the devil will doubtless be running his mouth, screaming from pain and suffering at the highest intensity level. He won't have time to think about you or anyone else as he forever undergo indescribable torments and torture which all become unbearably painful with each moment's breath.

Now back to Matthew 25, continuing with verse 42: **For I was an hungered, and ye gave Me no meat: I was thirsty, and ye gave Me no drink: I was a stranger, and ye took Me not in: naked, and ye clothed Me not: sick, and in prison, and ye visited Me not. Then shall they answer Him, saying, Lord, when saw we thee an hungered, or athirst, or a stranger, or naked, or sick, or in prison, and did not minister unto Thee? Then shall He answer them, saying, Verily I say unto you, Inasmuch as ye did it not to one of the least of these, ye did it not to Me. And these shall go away into everlasting punishment: but the righteous into life eternal** (Matt. 25:31-46).

Then shall two be in the field; the one shall be taken [into the judgment of everlasting punishment], **and the other left** [to remain on the earth to enter the Millennium period]. **Two women shall be grinding at the mill; the one shall be taken** [into the judgment of everlasting punishment]**, and the other left** [to remain on the earth to enter the Millennium period] (Matt. 24:40-41).

Once again, **"and He** (Jesus) **shall set the sheep on his right hand, but the goats on the left"** (Matt. 25:33). This separation is not arbitrary. The **"goats"** have the mark (666) of the beast and the **"sheep"** do not have the mark [Ref. Rev. 13:15-18].

Scripture explains: **And the third angel followed them, saying with a loud voice, if any man worship the beast and his image, and receive his mark in his forehead, or in his hand. The same shall drink of the wine of the wrath of God, which is poured out without mixture into the cup of his indignation; and he shall be tormented with fire and brimstone in the presence of the holy angels, and in the presence of the Lamb: And the smoke of their torment ascends up forever and ever: and they have no rest day nor night, who worship the beast and his image, and whosoever received the mark of his name. Here is the patience of the saints: here are they that keep the commandments of God, and the faith of Jesus. And I** (John) **heard a voice from heaven saying unto me, Write, Blessed are the dead** [namely the martyred tribulation saints] **which die in the Lord from henceforth: Yea, says the Spirit, that they may rest from their labors; and their works do follow them** (Rev. 14:9-13).

11

THE MILLENNIUM
(Rev. 20:1-6, Isaiah 11:1 –
12:6, 65:17-25)

And I saw an angel [perhaps Michael the archangel 12:7] **come down from heaven, having the key of the bottomless pit and a great chain in his hand. And he laid hold on the dragon, that old serpent, which is the Devil, and Satan, and bound him a thousand years. And cast him into the bottomless pit, and shut him up, and set a seal upon him, that he should deceive the nations no more till the thousand years should be fulfilled: and after that he must be loosed** (released) **a little season. And I saw thrones, and they** (Old Testament, New Testament & Church Age saints) **sat upon them, and judgment was given unto them: and I saw the souls of them** (Martyred saints) **that were beheaded for the witness of Jesus, and for the word of God, and which had not worshiped the beast, neither his image, neither had received his mark upon their foreheads, or in their hands; and they lived and reigned with Christ a thousand years. But the rest of the dead lived not again until the thousand years were finished. This is the**

first resurrection. Blessed and holy is he that hath part in the first resurrection: on such the second death hath no power, but they shall be priests of God and of Christ, and shall reign with Him a thousand years (Rev. 20:1-6).

The Millennium is the future time period when Jesus Christ and the saints of all ages will rule the world for one thousand years. Among several fulfillments, the Millennium will be the literal fulfillment of Jesus' teaching on the "model" prayer found in Matt. 6:10. Here Jesus prays to the Father, **Thy kingdom come. Thy will be done in earth, as it is in heaven.** Thus the New World Order and Prevailing Mindset during the Millennium, can be summed up in one verse: **Finally, brethren, whatsoever things are true, whatsoever things are honest, whatsoever things are just, whatsoever things are pure, whatsoever things are lovely, whatsoever things are of good report; if there be any virtue, and if there be any praise, think on these things** (Phil. 4:8).

In Daniel 7:26, God provides the prophet Daniel a sneak preview of the world's transition of power from darkness to light during this time: **But the judgment shall sit** [marking the end of the Antichrist's terror], **and they shall take away his dominion, to consume and to destroy it unto the end** [and never to recover]. **And the kingdom and dominion, and the greatness of the kingdom under the whole heaven, shall be given to the people of the saints of the most High** [referring to the Old & New Testament saints, the Church Age (Raptured) saints, the Tribulation & Martyred Saints—the saints of all ages], **whose kingdom is an everlasting kingdom,**

and all dominions shall serve and obey Him [referring to Jesus Christ; vs. 27].

In 1 Corinthians 6:2, the apostle Paul reminds the New Testament saints that they will reign with Christ and not only **judge the world** [during the Millennium] but will also **judge angels** [in the eternal state](vs. 3).

In Revelation 2:26, Jesus encourages the saints who were all raptured: **And he who overcomes, and keeps My works unto the end, to him I will give power over the nations.** And Timothy adds, **If we suffer, we shall also reign with Him** (2 Tim. 2:12).

And let's not forget the reign of the twelve apostles of the Lamb: **And Jesus said unto them, Verily I say unto you, That ye which have followed Me, in the regeneration when the Son of Man shall sit in the throne of His glory, ye also shall sit upon twelve thrones, judging the twelve tribes of Israel** (Matt. 19:28).

And finally, the Tribulation, Great Tribulation & martyred saints will all reign with Christ. **And I saw thrones, and they sat upon them, and judgment was given unto them: and I saw the souls of them that were beheaded for the witness of Jesus, and for the word of God, and which had not worshiped the beast, neither his image, neither had received his mark upon their foreheads, or in their hands: and they lived and reigned with Christ a thousand years** (Rev. 20:4).

We are reminded in Revelation 16 that GOD did not only use plagues to punish unrepentant sinners, but also used a great earthquake (v. 18) to cause **every island to flee away, and the mountains were not found** (v. 20). This dramatic changing of the earth's topography will prepare the earth for the millennial rule of Jesus Christ, and cause Jerusalem to be elevated as the highest point and most appropriate place for Him to rule during the Millennium. It's noteworthy to know that Jerusalem will not only be the highest point, but also the center point of the world.

When GOD created the heavens and the earth, He strategically placed Jerusalem at its center. Zechariah describes: **And it shall come to pass that every one that is left of all the nations which came against Jerusalem shall even go up from year to year to worship the King, the Lord of hosts, and to keep the feast of tabernacles. And it shall be, that whoso will not come up of all the families of the earth unto Jerusalem to worship the King, the Lord of hosts, even upon them shall be no rain. And if the family of Egypt go not up, and come not, that have no rain; there shall be the plague, wherewith the Lord will smite the heathen that come not up to keep the feast of tabernacles. This shall be the punishment of Egypt, and the punishment of all nations that come not up to keep the feast of tabernacles** (Zech. 14:16, 19). Thus the citizens from every nation will go UP to the city of Jerusalem which will become the earth's highest elevation point, strategically located in the center of the world. But that's not all. The punishment of no rain will be meted out to the citizens of all nations who fail to show up. WOW!!! WHAT DIVINE DICTATORSHIP . . . referring to Jesus Christ who **will rule them with a rod of iron** (Rev. 2:27), and all of us crazy Christians and martyred saints will be the enforcers of His rule (Rev. 20:4). Keep in mind, the

Feast of Tabernacles is just a 7-day annual event, and NOT a continuous 24/7, 365 days long CHURCH SERVICE. There should be NO EXCUSE for non-attendance. Thus any and all absentees will pay the penalty of **(no rain).**

Overall, during the millennium, life will be blissful with a wonderful paradise to enjoy. Satan and all of his evil influencers called demons are removed from the earth and bound for a thousand years in the bottomless pit (Rev. 20:1-3). Indeed, **the prince of the power of the air** [namely the airwaves of mainstream and social media], **the spirit that now works in the children of disobedience** [namely the God-rejecting rebels] (Eph. 2:2) is removed from the earth. The beast (Antichrist) and the false prophet are no longer a threat because **these both were cast alive into a lake of fire burning with brimstone** (Rev. 19:20b). And all of the God-rejecting sinners of all ages are presently **in hell** (Luke 16:23) and **being tormented with fire and in the presence of the holy angels** (Rev. 14:10), yet awaiting their final sentencing at **the great white throne of judgment** (Rev. 20:11-15).

Isaiah chapter 11:1 – 12:6 prophesy a glimpse of the promised UTOPIA called the Millennium: **And there shall come forth a rod** [Zech. 12:6] **out of the stem of Jesse** [Isa. 9:7], **and a Branch** [Isa. 4:2] **shall grow out of his roots: And the spirit of the Lord shall rest upon Him, the spirit of wisdom and understanding, the spirit of counsel and might, the spirit of knowledge and of the fear of the Lord** [referring to the sevenfold Spirit of God in Rev. 4:5 which describes His seven attributes]; **And shall make Him** (Jesus) **of quick understanding in the fear of the Lord: and He shall not judge after the sight** of His eyes, neither reprove after the hearing of His ears: But with righteousness (and having complete spiritual vision) shall He judge the poor, and reprove with equity for the meek of the earth: and He shall smite the earth with the rod of His mouth, and with the breath of His lips shall He slay the wicked [cf. Rev. 19:15]. And righteousness shall be the girdle of His loins, and faithfulness the girdle of His reins. The wolf also shall dwell with the lamb, and the leopard shall lie down with the kid; and the calf and the young lion and the fatling together; and a little child shall lead them. And the cow and the bear shall feed; their young ones shall lie down together: and the lion shall eat straw like the ox. And the sucking (small) child shall play on the hold of the asp (cobra), and the weaned child shall put his hand on the cockatrice' (viper's) den. They shall not hurt nor destroy in all My holy mountain; for the earth shall be full of the knowledge of the Lord, as the waters cover the sea [signifying that peace and harmony will extend even to the animal kingdom].

EVEN THE HOSTILE ENEMIES OF ISRAEL BECOME PEACEFUL

Shocking as it may seem, even the most hostile enemies of Israel will become peaceful. During the Millennium, Israel's most radical avid enemies will have an instant behavior change towards Israel, and resolve to live in peace with the Jews. Such a prospect will no doubt shock the conscience of most people, with the exception of Bible readers and Christmas celebrants. Each year, there are two verses which faithfully remind us: **For unto us a Child is born, unto us a Son is given: and the** government shall be upon His shoulder: and His name shall be called Wonderful, Counselor, The mighty God, The everlasting Father, The Prince of Peace. Of the increase of His government and peace there shall be no end, upon the throne of David, and upon His kingdom, to order it, and to establish it with judgment and with justice from henceforth even forever. The zeal of the Lord of hosts will perform this (Isa. 9:6,7).

Notably, **which in His times** (and during the Millennium) **He** (Jesus) **shall show, who is the blessed and only Potentate, the King of kings, and Lord of lords** (1 Tim. 6:15).

Isaiah 11:10 -16 continues: **And in that day there shall be a root of Jesse, which shall stand for an ensign** (standard) **of the** (Jewish) **people; to it shall the Gentiles seek: and His rest shall be glorious** [because this is the predicted time when salvation will come to both Jews and Gentiles]. **And it came to pass in that day, that the Lord shall set His hand again the second time to recover the remnant of the people, which shall be left, from Assyria** (to the north), **and from Egypt** (to the south), **and from Pathros** (upper Egypt), **and from Cush** (Ethiopia), **and from Elam** (the Persian Gulf), **and from Shinar** (Babylon), **and from Hamath** (on the Orontes River in Syria), **and from the islands of the sea. And He shall set up an ensign for the nations, and shall assemble the outcasts of Israel, and gather together the dispersed of Judah from the four corners of the earth. The envy also of Ephraim shall depart, and the adversaries of Judah shall be cut off: Ephraim shall not envy Judah, and Judah shall not vex Ephraim. But they shall fly upon the shoulders of the Philistines toward the west; they shall spoil them of the east together: they shall lay their hand**

upon Edom and Moab: and the Children of Ammon shall
obey them. And the Lord shall utterly destroy the tongue of
the Egyptian sea; and with the mighty wind shall He shake
His hand over the river, and shall smite it in the seven streams,
and make them go dryshod (and easy to be passed over). And
there shall be a highway for the remnant of His people, which
shall be left, from Assyria; like as it was to Israel in the day
that He came up out of the land of Egypt.

Isaiah chapter 12: 1-6 continues: **And in that day** (cf. Isa. 2:11)
**thou shalt say, O Lord, I will praise thee: though thou was
angry with me, thine anger is turned away, and thou comforted me. Behold, God is my salvation; I will trust, and not
be afraid: for the LORD JEHOVAH is my strength and my
song; He is also become my salvation. Therefore with joy
shall ye draw water out of the wells of salvation. And in that
day shall ye say, Praise the Lord, call upon His name, declare
His doings among the people, make mention that His name
is exalted. Sing unto the Lord** [as Moses and the children
of Israel did after crossing the Red Sea on dry ground. [Ref.
Exodus 14:21 – 15;21] **for He hath done excellent things: this
is known in all the earth. Cry out** (cf. Isa. 52:9), **and shout,
thou inhabitant of Zion: for great is the Holy One of Israel
in the midst of thee.**

NEW HEAVENS & A NEW EARTH
(Isaiah 65:17-25)

For, behold I (Jesus) **create new heavens and a new earth** (cf.
Rev. 21): **and the former shall not be remembered, nor come**

into mind. **But be ye glad and rejoice forever in that which I create: for behold, I create Jerusalem a rejoicing, and her people a joy. And I will rejoice in Jerusalem, and joy in my people: and the voice of weeping shall be no more heard in her, nor the voice of crying** [especially from terrorists' attacks]. **There shall be no more thence an infant of days** [who lives but a few days; no miscarriages, no stillbirths], **nor an old man that hath not filled his days: for the child shall die a hundred years old** [which will be thought of as dying young], **but the sinner being a hundred years old shall be accursed** [which means that even under the penalty of guilt, the sinner will live to at least a hundred years old]. **And they shall build houses, and inhabit them** [because there will be no crises or setbacks]. **And they shall plant vineyards, and eat the fruit of them** [because there will be no natural disasters or crop-destroying insects]. **They shall not build, and another inhabit** [as a result of being jobless or encountering misfortune]; **they shall not plant, and another eat** [the fruits of their labor]: **for as the days of a tree are the days of my people, and mine elect shall long enjoy the work of their hands** [with no adversity or affliction]. **They shall not labor in vain** [due to crop failure, futility or plunder], **nor bring forth for trouble** [because there will be no natural disastrous plagues, storms, hurricanes, tornadoes or pandemics]. **For they are the seed of the blessed of the Lord, and their offspring** (children) **with them. And it shall come to pass, that before they call, I will answer; and while they are yet speaking, I will hear** [showing the Lord's readiness to assist His people in any way]. **The wolf and the lamb shall feed together, and the lion shall eat straw like the bullock** (or young bull): **and dust shall be the serpent's meat** (food). **They shall not hurt nor destroy**

in all my holy mountain, saith the Lord [because worldwide peace will encompass even the animal kingdom].

In summary, Apostle Paul reminds us: **For the earnest expectation of the creature** (creation) **waits for the manifestation of the sons of God … For we know that the whole creation groans and travails in pain until now** (Romans 8:19,22). Adam's Fall (Genesis 3:1-24) has caused so much misery, pain and suffering in this world from then until now. In the Millennium, the curse will be lifted and life will be elongated and blissful. You won't even get a headache because someone has gotten on your nerves. No anxiety. No stress. No disappointment. No hurt. No pain. Can you say, "UTOPIA"?

UTOPIA indeed, but not for everyone!

Even in a perfect environment, **the sheep on His right hand** (Matt. 25:33) will enter the Millennium kingdom as flesh and blood and repopulate the earth. They and their offspring all will still have a sinful nature. And some will choose not to **seek first the kingdom of God, and His righteousness** (Matt. 6:33). You may ask how could this happen? Well, the answer can be summed up in one word: CARNALITY. The Apostle Paul reminds us: **For they that are after the flesh do mind the things of the flesh; but they that are after the Spirit the things of the Spirit. For to be carnally** (worldly) **minded is death; but to spiritually minded is life and peace.** And here's the clincher. **Because the carnal mind is enmity against God** [even in a perfect environment]: **For it is not subject to the law of God, neither indeed can be. So then that that are in the flesh cannot please God** [without surrendering their lives to Jesus Christ]. **But ye** (saints) **are not in the flesh, but in the Spirit, if so be that the Spirit of God dwell in you. Now if any man** (or person) **have not the Spirit of Christ, he is none of His** (Romans 8:5-9).

In the Millennium, sin will continue. Crime will exist. Laws will be broken. However, any and all wrongdoing will face swift and just punishment because Jesus [again] **shall rule them with a rod of iron** (Rev. 2:27), and His saints will enforce His rule all over the world (Rev. 20:6). Here King David exclaims:

Why do the heathen rage, and the people imagine a vain thing? The kings of the earth set themselves, and the rulers take counsel together, against the Lord, and against His Anointed, saying, Let us break their bands asunder, and cast away their cords from us. He that sits in the heaven shall laugh: the Lord shall have them in derision. Then shall He speak unto them in His wrath, and vex them in sore displeasure. Yet have I set my King upon my holy hill of Zion. I will declare the decree: The Lord hath said unto me, Thou art my Son; this day have I begotten thee. Ask of me, and I shall give thee the heathen for Thine inheritance, and the uttermost parts of the earth for Thy possession. Thou shalt break them with a rod of iron; thou shalt dash them in pieces like a pot-ter's vessel. Be wise now therefore, O ye kings: be instructed, ye judges of the earth. Serve the Lord with fear, and rejoice with trembling. Kiss the Son (Reverence Jesus Christ), **lest He be angry, and ye perish from the way, when His wrath is kindled but a little. Blessed are all they that put their trust in Him** (Ps. 2:1-12).

KINGS AND PRIESTS

And hath made us kings and priests unto our God and His Father; to Him be glory and dominion for ever and ever. Amen (Rev. 1:6). In reference to "kings", this particular verse now brings us to the "parable of the ten pounds" mentioned in Luke 19: He (Jesus) **said therefore, a certain nobleman went into a far country to receive for himself a kingdom, and to return. And he called his ten servants, and delivered them ten pounds, and said unto them, Occupy** (do business or trade) **till I come . . . And it came to pass, that when He** (Jesus) **was returned, having received the** (Millennium) **kingdom, then He commanded His servants to be called unto Him, to whom He had given the money** (resources), **that He might know how much every man had gained by trading. Then came the first, saying, Lord, thy pound hath gained ten pounds. And He said unto him, Well, thou good servant: because thou hast been faithful in a very little, have thou authority** [as a king] **over ten cities** [during the Millennium] (Luke 19:12-13, 15-17). **And the second came, saying, Lord, thy pound hath gained five pounds. And He said likewise to him, Be thou also** [as a king] **over five cities** (Luke 19:18, 19) during the Millennium.

A companion passage is "the parable of the talents" to be found in Matthew 25: 15, 20-23. **For the kingdom of heaven is as a man traveling into a far country, who called his own servants, and delivered unto them his goods. And unto one He** (Jesus) **gave five talents, to another two, and to another one; to every man according to his several ability; and straightway took His journey . . . And so he that received five talents came and brought other five talents, saying, Lord, thou delivered**

unto me five talents: behold, I have gained beside them five talents more. His lord said unto him, Well done thou good and faithful servant: thou hast been faithful over a few things, I will make thee ruler over many things: enter thou into the joy of thy Lord. And in verses 22 and 23, the same commendation and rewards were also given to the one who gained two other talents. Jesus would also appoint that person to be a ruler in the Millennium kingdom.

Now concerning **"making others priests unto our God"** during the Millennium kingdom, Zechariah explains: **Thus says the Lord of hosts; It shall yet come to pass, that there shall come people, and the inhabitants of many cities: And the inhabitants of one city shall go to another, saying, Let us go speedily** (continually) **before the Lord, and to seek the Lord of hosts: I will go also. Yea, many people and strong nations shall come to seek the Lord of hosts in Jerusalem, and to pray before the Lord. Thus says the Lord of hosts; In those days it shall come to pass** [as priests unto our God], **that ten men shall take hold out of all languages of the nations, even shall take hold of the skirt of him that is a Jew, saying, We will go with you: for we have heard that God is with you** (Zech. 8:20-23).

When scripture declares that **"ten men shall take hold out of all languages of the nations"**, I'm reminded of 1 Corinthians 13:12 which states: **For now we** (saints) **see through a glass darkly** (or dimly); **but then face to face: now I** (Apostle Paul) **know in part: but then shall I know even as also I am known.**

Because we are glorified, our knowledge will become exponential, but limited (like angels) [Ref. 1 Peter 1:12]. GOD ALONE

IS OMNISCIENT. However, during the Millennium and the Eternal State, everything we need to know, WE WILL KNOW because **we have an unction from the Holy One, and we know all things** (1 John 2:20)– that being, all things we will need to know will be those very things we will know. No introduction. No language barriers. No counselor. At that time, I believe that **we** saints will literally **have the mind of Christ** (1 Cor. 2:16), and yet retain our individual personalities. And that's not all.

Do you remember what happened at Pentecost? The outpouring of the Holy Spirit caused all attendees **to speak with other tongues, as the Spirit gave them utterance. And there was dwelling at Jerusalem Jews, devout men, out of every nation under the heaven. Now when this was noised abroad, the multitude came together, and were confounded, because that every man heard them speak in his own language. And they were all amazed and marveled, saying one to another, Behold, are not all these which speak Galileans? And how is it that we hear, each in our own language in which we were born** (Acts 2:4-8)? It bears repeating: There will be no language barriers among "glorified" saints because all of us will **have an unction from the Holy one, and we know all things** (1 Cor. 2:16). WHAT A THRILL it will be for us to have a fluent conversation in a language we never learned! HEAVEN IS MORE THAN AMAZING! Scripture reminds us, **"But as it is written, eye has not seen, nor ear heard, neither have entered into the heart of man, the things which God has prepared for those who love Him** (1 Cor. 2:9).

MORE THAN A SUPERHERO!

During the Millennium and the Eternal State, Christians will possess divine powers more spectacular than their favorite superhero. Mankind has always desired to conquer and to be limitless; to be powerful and invincible; to be triumphant and immortal. Having glorified bodies, the Millennium period will be our debut to display our "superhuman" abilities. Just imagine travelling at the speed of thought. We will be able to appear, disappear and reappear at whim (cf. John 20:19-20). No flight reservations. No car rentals. No rockets. No space suit. No wetsuit. Vacation for us will be exploring other planets and galaxies—all of God's glorious creation, even at the speed of thought. We will be transcendent, operating beyond or above the range of normal or physical human experience.

Today's superheroes (no matter how heroic or how creative the human mind can conjure) will always be subject to the limitations of the material universe. However, those limitations will not apply to us Christians. Like Jesus, every believer enters spiritual warfare. **"Our adversary the devil"**(1 Pet. 5:8) desires to kill us all [especially Jesus] in order to thwart God's plan of the ages. In chapter 5 of this book, we read that after king "Herod the Great" in his conspiracy to kill the baby Jesus, discovered that he was duped by the wise men who **"were warned of God in a dream that they should not return to Herod"** (Matt. 2:12), he no doubt went berserk and ordered the killing of all the children **"from two years old and under"** (vs. 16). Even at the outset of Jesus' earthly ministry, the devil tried to kill Him once again. At this time, however, it was at the hands of the angry religious mob:

And He (Jesus) came to Nazareth, where He had been
brought up: and, as His custom was, He went into the syn-
agogue on the Sabbath day, and stood up for to read. And
there was delivered unto Him the book of the prophet Isaiah.
And when He had opened the book, He found the place
where it was written, THE SPIRITOF THE LORD IS
UPON ME, BECAUSE HE HATH ANOINTED ME TO
PREACH THE GOSPEL TO THE POOR; HE HATH
SENT ME TO HEAL THE BROKEN-HEARTED,
TO PREACH DELIVERANCE TO THE CAPTIVES,
AND RECOVERING OF SIGHT TO THE BLIND, TO
SET AT LIBERTY THEM THAT ARE BRUISED, TO
PREACH THE ACCEPTABLE YEAR OF THE LORD.
And He closed the book, and He gave it again to the min-
ister, and sat down. And the eyes of all them that were in
the synagogue were fastened on Him. And He (The Son of
God in His humanity) began to say unto them, this day is
this scripture fulfilled in your ears. And all bare Him wit-
ness, and wondered at the gracious words which proceeded
out of His mouth. And they said, is not this Joseph's son? And
He said unto them, you will surely say unto Me this proverb,
Physician, heal Thyself: whatsoever we have heard done in
Capernaum, do also here in thy country. And He said, Verily
I say unto you, No prophet is accepted in his own country. But
I tell you of a truth, many widows were in Israel in the days
of Elijah, when the heaven was shut up three years and six
months, when great famine was throughout all the land; But
unto none of them was Elijah sent, save unto Sarepta, a city
of Sidon, unto a woman that was a widow. And many lepers
were in Israel in the time of Elisha the prophet: and none of
them was cleansed, saving Naaman the Syrian. And all they

in the synagogue, when they heard these things, were filled with wrath, And rose up, and thrust Him out of the city, and led Him unto the brow (cliff) of the hill whereon their city was built, that they may cast Him down headlong. But He (God the Son in His Divinity) passing through the midst of them went His way (Luke 4:16-30). PLEASE READ THE LAST SENTENCE AGAIN.

Jesus lived on planet earth as the God/Man. He is 100% GOD; He is 100% man. And in the heat of conflict, Jesus did not transform into "Iron Man", pick up a sword, become a whirlwind, and obliterate every enemy. Instead, I believe while Jesus was in the very grip of the angry religious mobsters, He instantly transitioned from humanity to deity and passed through their physical bodies to safety. Can you say, THEOPHANY? His enemies (no doubt) exclaimed and said to one another, "What on earth just happened?" We had Him in our very grips and He passes through us like a ghost. Needless to say, they did not sleep well that night!

Here's a verse to remember: For the Son of Man did not come to destroy men's lives, but to save them (Luke 9:56). Yet scripture reveals other satanic attempts on the life of Jesus, and while I have your attention, let me share one more episode. The scripture passage is found in John chapter 8 when Jesus claimed, "Before Abraham was, I am" (vs. 58). Jesus tells the Jews, "Verily, verily, I say unto you, if a man keep my saying, he shall never see death. Then said the Jews unto Him, now we know that You have a devil. Abraham is dead, and the prophets; and You say, if a man keep my saying, he shall never taste of death. Are You greater than our father Abraham, who is dead? And the prophets are dead: Who do You make Yourself out to be? Jesus answered, if I honor myself, my honor is nothing. It is My Father who honors Me, of Whom you say that He is your God. Yet you have not known Him, but I know Him. And if I say, 'I do not know Him,' I shall be a liar like you; but I do know Him and keep His word. Your father Abraham rejoiced to see My day, and he saw it and was glad. Then the Jews said unto Him, "You are not yet fifty years old, and have You seen Abraham?" Jesus said unto them, "Most assuredly, I say to you, before Abraham was, I AM." Then they took up stones to throw at Him; but Jesus hid Himself and went out of the temple, going through the midst of them, and so passed by (John 8:51-59). And, in the words of MC Hammer: "U CAN'T TOUCH THIS!"

Jesus reminds us, "Therefore my Father loves Me, because I lay down My life that I may take it again. No one takes it from Me, but I lay it down, and I have power to take it again. This command I have received from My Father (Jn. 10:17, 18).

During the Millennium period, His citizen will not only hate Him, but hate us "Enforcers" of His righteous rule all the more. At that time, murder and assassination attempts on us "glorified" Christians will just be futile thoughts, and impossible to accomplish because we will be immortal and have supernatural abilities that exceed even those abilities of our favorite superheroes.

As such, it's to be duly noted that GOD will be known by the judgments He and His saints strictly execute worldwide. He will lay nothing upon His citizens but what is for their good. Nonetheless, **His citizens will hate Him, and send a message**

after Him, saying, we will not have this man to reign over us (Luke 19:14). And after the end of the Millennium, all Christ-rejecting sinners worldwide who stubbornly resist His righteous authority will join with Satan for the final world war.

12

WORLD WAR IV
(Revelation 20:7-10)

SATAN'S FINAL REBELLION AND ETERNAL BANISHMENT TO HELL / GOG & MAGOG PART 2

And when the thousand years are expired (and completed), **Satan shall be loosed out of his prison, and shall go out to deceive** [with that same spirit that now works in the children of disobedience – Eph. 2:2] **the nations** [all over the globe] **which are in the four quarters of the earth, Gog** (a renowned human leader) **and Magog** (his army of followers), **to gather them together to battle** [for the final war in human history]: **the** (innumerable) **number of whom is as the sand of the sea** [due to extended human life spans and massive population growth during the Millennium]. **And they went up on the breath of the earth, and compassed the camp of the saints about, and the beloved city** [Jerusalem which is the world's central head-quarter]: **and fire came down from God out of heaven, and devoured them.** In other words, Satan's final attempt to defeat

Christ instantly goes up in FLAMES. **And the devil that deceived them was cast into the lake of fire and brimstone, where the beast and the false prophet are, and shall be tormented day and night for ever and ever** (Rev. 20:10).

Here we see Satan, who is the epitome of all evil, being released from his prison and return to the earth with the most hateful vengeance (unimaginable). Just like an incorrigible child, the more you punish and beat him, the madder he gets. And returning as **the god of this world,** Satan will easily **blind the minds of them which believe not** (2 Cor. 4:4). His selection pool will be worldwide as he enlists all those **citizens that hated Jesus Christ** [and His righteous rule] **and who sent a message after Him saying, we will not have this man to reign over us** [during the Millennium period](Luke 19:14). Once again, Satan is GOD's devil. And at this final conflict in world history, GOD will ultimately use Satan [one last time] to enlist all those enemies of God who despised His righteous rule and never wanted Him to reign over them, to be slain instantly before Him (Luke 19:27 paraphrased). We read, **and fire came down from God out of heaven, and devoured them** (Rev. 20:9b).

Who are these people? Do you remember the judgment of nations? Well, after World War III which is the Battle of Armageddon, **Jesus sat upon the throne of His glory: And before Him was gathered all nations :** [Keep in mind that citizens don't go to war, but do become subjects of the new ruling authorities].**and Jesus separated them one from another, as a shepherd divides his sheep from the goats: He set the sheep** [not having the mark of the beast (cf. Rev. 13:16,17) **on His right hand, but the goats** [having the mark of the beast] **on the**

left. Then the King said unto them on His right hand, Come, ye blessed of my Father, inherit the kingdom prepared for you from the foundation of the world (Matt. 25:31-34).

So these people are the survivors of the Tribulation and Great Tribulation who enter the Millennium kingdom in their normal physical "flesh and blood" bodies. They will still have a sinful human nature and repopulate the earth on an exponential scale via marriage and fornication. And although various business operations will continue worldwide, Plan Parenthood and all abortion clinics will not exist during the Millennium.

John MacArthur, Jr. aptly explains the social conditions and eventual apathy at this time:

"Though the initial inhabitants of the millennial kingdom will all be redeemed, they will still possess a sinful human nature. And as all parents have done since the Fall, they will pass that sin nature on to their offspring. Each successive generation throughout the thousand years will be made up of sinners in need of salvation. Many will come to saving faith in the Lord Jesus Christ. But amazingly, despite the personal rule of Christ on earth, despite the most moral society the world will ever know, many others will love their sin and reject Him (cf. Rom. 8:7). Even the utopian conditions of the Millennium will not change the sad reality of human depravity. As they did during the incarnational presence on earth, sinners will refuse the grace and reject the lordship of the King of all the earth. That is not surprising, since even the perfect conditions of the Garden of Eden were not sufficient to keep sinless Adam and Eve from rebelling against God. The issue regarding salvation is never lack of information (cf. Rom.1:18-20); it is love of sin (John 3:19). Those who openly rebel will face swift judgment (2:27; 12:5; 19:15; Ps. 2:9), including the withholding of rain on their land (Zech. 14:16-19). But enough unrepentant sinners will be alive at the end of the Millennium for Satan to lead a world-wide rebellion.

When Satan is loosed, he will provide cohesive supernatural leadership needed to bring to the surface all the latent sin and rebellion left in the universe. He will put together all the rebels, revealing the true character and intent of those Christ-rejecting sinners and making it evident that God's judgment of them is just. Satan's desperate wickedness and violent hatred of God and Christ will not be altered by his thousand years of imprisonment in the abyss. When he is released, he will immediately set about fomenting his final act of rebellion"(The MacArthur New Testament Commentary, Revelation 12-22, pp. 239,240).

So while all of us Saints are hanging out in Jerusalem and enjoying the presence of Christ in all His Glory, we will find ourselves totally surrounded by a massive swarm of enemies who are all poised and ready to attack. Without question, their minds have been blinded by Satan [Ref. 2 Cor. 4:4], rendering them totally oblivious to 2 Chronicles 20:15: **And He** (GOD) **said, Hearken** (listen) **ye, all Judah, and ye inhabitants of Jerusalem, and thou King Jehoshaphat, Thus says the LORD unto you, Be not afraid nor dismayed by reason of this great multitude; for the battle is not yours, but God's. "And fire came down from God out of heaven, and devoured them"** (Rev. 20:9b). THE FINAL BATTLE IN WORLD HISTORY IS

OVER IN AN INSTANT! And we are soberly reminded of two key scriptures:

1) **For our God is a consuming fire** (Heb. 12:29).

2) **It is a fearful** (dreadful) **thing to fall into the hands of the living God** (Heb. 10:31).

God's Word is His Power

Please understand this truth: We cannot separate GOD from His speech. Hebrews 1:3 reminds us that GOD **upholds all things by the word of His power,** and not by the power of His word. If GOD upheld all things by the power of His word, there may not be enough power in His word to get the job done. Scripture is clear. GOD upholds all things by the word of His power, signifying that GOD'S WORD IS HIS POWER. Because GOD cannot be separated from His speech, here are a few verses to affirm this truth:

God is not a man, that He should lie; neither the son of man, that He should repent: hath He said, and shall He not do it? Or hath He spoken, and shall He not make good (Num. 23:19)?

In hope of eternal life, which God, that cannot lie, promised before the world began (Titus 1:2);

That by two immutable things, in which it was impossible for God to lie, we might have a strong consolation, who have fled for refuge to lay hold upon the hope set before us (Heb. 6:18):

The grass withers, the flower fades: but the word of God shall stand forever (Isa. 40:8).

The counsel of the Lord stands forever, the thoughts of His heart to all generations (Ps. 33:11).

For truly I tell you, until heaven and earth disappear, not the smallest letter (one jot), not the least stroke of a pen (one tittle), will by any means disappear (or pass away) from the Law until everything is accomplished. Therefore anyone who sets aside one of the least of these commands and teaches others accordingly will be called least in the kingdom of heaven, but whoever practices and teaches these commands will be called great in the kingdom of heaven (Matt. 5:18,19 NIV).

Continuing in Revelation 20:10, And the devil that deceived them was cast into the lake of fire and brimstone, where the beast (Anti-Christ) and the false prophet are, and shall be tormented day and night forever and ever [without a moment's relief].

13

THE GREAT WHITE THRONE OF JUDGMENT
(Rev. 20:11-15)

And I saw a great white throne , and Him [THE UNCAUSED CAUSE & THE UNMOVED MOVER] **that sat on it, from whose face the earth and the heaven fled away; and there was found no place for them. And I saw the dead, small and great,** [low and high, young and old, rich and poor] **stand before God; and the books were opened: and another book was opened, which is the book of life: and the dead were judged out of those things which were written in the books, according to their works. And the sea gave up the dead which were in it; and death** [which has the body] **and hell** [which has the soul] **delivered up the dead which were in them** [signifying that the state of a person's physical body after death has nothing to do with their eternal destiny]: In relation to creation, **God spoke and it was done; He commanded and it stood fast** (Ps. 33:9). God can remake (Gen. 1:26a) or reassemble and resurrect a person whether their body was buried, cremated, drowned in the sea, or blown up in pieces: **and they were judged every man according to their works.** The persons to be judged are the unrighteous dead which **were cast into the lake of fire. This is the second** (or eternal) **death. And whosoever was not found written in the book of life was cast into the lake of fire** (Rev. 20:11-15).

We now come to the most serious, the most sobering, the most dreadful and tragic event in human history: The Great White Throne of Judgment. And before we delve into it, we're reminded of the two resurrections prophesied by the prophet Daniel: **And many of them that sleep in the dust of the earth shall awake, some to everlasting life, and some to shame and everlasting contempt** (Dan. 12:2). The first resurrection is mentioned in Revelation 20:4 to include the raptured saints, the martyred saints, and the saints of all ages. **"This is the first resurrection. Blessed and holy is the one who shares in the first resurrection! Over such the second death has no power, but they will be priests of God and of Christ, and they will reign with Him for a thousand years"** (Rev. 20:5b-6). Remember those who were involved in the first resurrection will already be raised to life prior to the 1,000-year reign of Christ called the Millennium. The second resurrection (described in Revelation 20:12-13) will occur after the Millennium. **And I saw the dead, small and great, stand before God . . . and they were judged every man according to their works.**

WHO IS SITTING ON THE GREAT WHITE THRONE?

Speaking to the Jews, the Apostle Paul explains, **"Because He** (God The Father) **has appointed a day, in the which He will**

judge the world in righteousness by that man (Jesus Christ) **whom He has ordained; whereof He** (The Father) **had given assurance unto all men, in that He had raised Him** (Jesus Christ) **from the dead"** (Acts 17:31). Thus He who sits on the throne is none other than the Lord Jesus Christ Himself.

During His earthly ministry, Jesus would often describe His unique relationship with the Father, especially in John 5:17-30. **Therefore the Jews sought the more to kill Him, because He not only had broken the Sabbath, but said also that God was His Father, making Himself equal with God** (vs. 18). In this same passage, Jesus explains, **For the Father judges no one, but has committed all judgment to the Son, that all should honor the Son just as they honor the Father. He who does not honor the Son, does not honor the Father who sent Him** (vss.22.23). Thus the very One whom sinners reject is the very One who will judge them.

SAVIOR OR JUDGE?

We can meet Jesus Christ now as OUR SAVIOR or meet Him then as OUR JUDGE. Meet Him, WE MUST!

At this last courtroom in human history, we find all the God-rejecting, unsaved people who have ever lived stand before GOD **from whose face the earth and the heaven fled away, and there was found no place for them** (vs. 11). Remember in Matthew 24:35, Jesus promised, **Heaven and earth shall pass away, but my words shall not pass away.** We've now come to the fulfillment of that promise. Other reference scriptures for this "fleeting" world are Ps. 102:25, 26; Isa. 51:6; Luke 21:33; Heb. 12:26,27.

In this last courtroom, there will be no bailiff, no jury, no character witness, no defense attorney, no cross examination, no plea deal, no parole board – only the All-knowing and All-seeing Prosecutor & Supreme Judge of the whole universe. Scripture reminds us, **and there is no creature hidden from His sight, but all things are naked and open to the eyes of Him to Whom we must give account** (Heb. 4:13). **He is the Rock, His work is perfect; For all His ways are judgment** [and He will adjudicate the most accurate justice]: **A God of truth and without iniquity, just and right is He** (Deut.32:4).

But you thought everyone could live as they please; you thought everyone could do what was right in their own eyes; you thought you could sin as much and as often as you so desired, and continue without consequence. You thought when you die, you're DONE. Life is all over: No Afterlife. And you simply pass into a state of annihilation, thereby ceasing to exist. No Ultimate Accountability. No Future Punishment.

And if the Devil could, he would yet laugh at your spiritual blindness and willful ignorance. But, of course at this time, Satan is "forever" hollering and screaming as he constantly experiences the most excruciating "pain and suffering" inflicted by GOD at its highest intensity. His being **"cast into the lake of fire and brimstone"** will not allow Satan [for even a moment] to laugh, grin or smile.

DO YOU WANT TO GO TO HEAVEN?

To go to heaven, we all must be sinless--100% perfect, 100% of the time. And GOD, knowing that such a prospect would be **impossible with men** (Luke 18:27), **gave His only begotten Son, that whosoever believes in Him should not perish** [go to hell], **but have everlasting life** [enter heaven] (John 3:16). As Savior, **God was in Christ, reconciling the world unto Himself, not imputing** (or adding up) **their trespasses to them, and has committed to us the word of reconciliation** (2 Cor. 5:9). **For as in Adam all die, even so in Christ shall all be made alive** (1 Cor. 15:22).

In Isaiah 53, we read a prophecy of GOD's purpose and plight for Jesus as the suffering servant:

Who has believed our report? And to whom has the arm of the LORD been revealed? For He shall grow up before Him as a tender plant, And as a root out of dry ground. He has no form or comeliness; And when we see Him, There is no beauty that we should desire Him. He is despised and rejected by men, A Man of sorrows and acquainted with grief. And we hid, as it were, our faces from Him; He was despised, and we did not esteem Him. Surely He has borne our grief and carried our sorrows; Yet we esteemed Him stricken, smitten of God, and afflicted. But He was wounded for our transgressions, He was (bruised and) **buried for our iniquities; The chastisement for our peace was upon Him, And by His stripes we are healed. All we like sheep have gone astray; We have turned, every one, to his own way; And the Lord has laid on Him the iniquity of us all. He was oppressed and He was afflicted, Yet He**

opened not His mouth; He was led as a lamb to the slaughter, and as sheep before its shears is silent, So He opened not His mouth. He was taken from prison and from judgment, And who will declare His generation? For He was cut off from the land of the living; For the transgressions of My people He was stricken. And they made His grave with the wicked— But with the rich at His death, Because He had done no violence, Nor was any deceit in His mouth. Yet it pleased the LORD to bruise Him; He has put Him to grief. When You make His soul an offering for sin, He shall see His seed, He shall prolong His days, And the pleasure of the LORD shall prosper in His hand. He shall see the labor of His soul, and be satisfied. By His knowledge My righteous Servant shall justify many, For He shall bear their iniquities. Therefore I will divide Him a portion with the great, And He shall divide the spoil with the strong, Because He poured out His soul unto death, And He was numbered with the transgressors, And He bore the sin of many, and made intercession for the transgressors (Isa. 53:1-12).

This undeserved suffering was so awful that even King David had to express his concurring wish list in Psalm 69. Speaking of the suffering Christ, he would lament, **Reproach has broken my heart; and I am full of heaviness: and I looked for some to take pity, but there was none; and comforters, but I found none. They gave me also gall for my meat; and in my thirst they gave me vinegar to drink. Let their table become a snare before them: and that which should have been for their welfare, let it become a trap. Let their eyes be darkened, that they see not, and make their loins (thighs) continually to shake. Pour out thy indignation upon them, and let thy wrathful** anger take hold of them. Let their habitation be desolate; and let none dwell in their tents. For they persecute him whom thou hast smitten; and they talk grief of those whom thou hast wounded. Add iniquity unto their iniquity: and let them not come into thy righteousness. Let them be blotted out of the book of the living, and not be written with the righteous (Ps. 69:20-28).

BOTTOMLINE: GOD does not exact double payment for any sin! **Christ has redeemed us from the curse of the law, being made a curse for us: for it is written, Cursed is everyone who hangs on a tree** (Gal. 3:13). We can receive Jesus Christ today as SAVIOR and accept His payment for our sins. Or, we can personally face Him as JUDGE, and eternally pay for our sins.

LIFE IS CHOICE-DRIVEN.

We can choose our neighborhoods, schools, restaurants, clubs, spouses, vehicles, friends, vacation, sports, transportation, entertainment, pets, activities, leisure, etc. When we add up the sum of all choices we made in this life, there's only one choice that matters eternally: What did you do with Jesus Christ? Is He your Savior? Or will He be your Judge?

At the Great White Throne of Judgment, every sin, every mistake, every infraction, every word (and slip of the tongue), every deed, every misdeed and even **every secret** (Rom. 2:16) will all be judged, because **the books** [of every sinner's biography] **were opened: and another book was opened, which is the book of life: and the dead were judged out of those things which were written in the books, according to their works** [signifying that the degree of each one's eternal punishment will be tailored-made according to his or her deeds]. No appeal. No do-overs. No rehabilitation.

Seldom known to most, it's critical to note that sinners and saints alike are both servants of God: And the Lord said, **Who then is that faithful and wise steward, whom His lord shall make ruler over His household, to give them their portion of meat in due season? Blessed is that servant, whom His lord when he comes shall find so doing. Of a truth I say unto you, that He will make him ruler over all that He has. But if that servant shall say in his heart, my Lord delays His coming; and shall begin to beat the menservants and maidens, and to eat and drink, and to be drunken. The lord of that servant will come in a day when he is not looking for Him, and at an hour when he is not aware, and will cut him in two and appoint him his portion with the unbelievers. And that servant who knew His master's will, and prepared not himself, neither did according to His will, shall be beaten with many stripes. But he who knew not, and did commit things worthy of stripes, shall be beaten with few stripes. For unto whomsoever much is given, of him shall be much required: and to whom men have committed much, of him they will ask the more** (Luke 12:42-48).

The companion text for this passage gets even more specific in the book of Matthew. Here **"the servant who knew His master's will, and prepared not himself"** is also identified as **"that evil servant"** who says in his heart, my master is delaying his coming, and begin to smite (beat) **his fellow servants, and to eat and drink with the drunkards, the master of that servant** will come on a day when he is not looking for Him and at an hour that he is not aware of, and will cut him in two and appoint him his portion with the hypocrites. There shall be weeping and gnashing of teeth (Matt. 24:48-50).

ARE YOU STILL PAYING ATTENTION? If you're tired at this point, go ahead and get some rest. And when you return, a special seat will be reserved for you at the front of the class.

Now let's continue. All the unbelievers and hypocrites in human history will face Jesus Christ as JUDGE at the Great White Throne of Judgment. The Bible refers to this most dreadful event as the **resurrection of damnation for all those who have done evil** (John 5:29b) and their resurrection **to shame and everlasting contempt** (Dan. 12:2b).

DON'T GAMBLE WITH ETERNITY

When the Father tells His Son that it's time to get His bride, the church is raptured and **"meets the Lord in the air"** (1 Thes. 4:17) and is saved from the wrath to come. As scripture puts it, **"Much more then, having being justified by His blood, we shall be saved from wrath through Him** (Rom. 5:9). After millions of Christians have 'all of a sudden' vanished from the earth, many "Smarter than God" unbelievers may conclude that it's now time to get saved and give their lives to the Lord because they remember hearing or even reading about The Rapture in the Bible.

NOT SO FAST, my friend. If you were not raptured, you will then experience GOD's wrath. The "Grace" period is now over.

Before the rapture, scripture is clear: **For by grace, you have been saved through faith. And this is not your own doing** [and you cannot take credit for it]; **It is the gift of God: Not of works, lest any man should boast** (Eph. 2:8-9). After the church is raptured, you cannot just willy-nilly choose the Savior after a lifetime of clinging to your sin and rejecting His Son. The Bible reminds us, **"no one can come to Me unless the Father who sent Me draws him; and I (Jesus) will raise him up on the last day** (John 6:44). Furthermore, at this time, **God will send them strong delusion, that they should believe a lie that they all may be damned** [and condemned] **who did not believe the truth but had pleasure in unrighteousness** (2 Thes. 2:11).

During this most dreadful time in world history, The Lord guarantees that only the Jews of the flesh will be saved, and not all the Gentiles [referring to the lost people]: **Alas, for that day is great, so that none is like it: it is even the time of Jacob's trouble; but he shall be saved out of it** (Jer. 30:7). **And so all Israel shall be saved: as it is written, there shall come out of Zion the Deliverer, and shall turn away ungodliness from Jacob: For this is my covenant unto them, when I shall take away their sins** (Romans 11:26-27).

My friend, unless you're a Jew of the flesh, I implore you NOT to gamble with eternity during your lifetime. Scripture is emphatic: **And as it is appointed unto men once to die, but after this the judgment: So Christ was once offered to bear the sins of many; and unto them that look for Him shall He appear the second time without sin unto salvation** (Heb. 9:27-28). So choosing the Savior today will deliver you from God's judgment at death. **For He says: In an acceptable time**

I have heard you, And in the day of salvation [and under Grace] **I have helped you. Behold now is the accepted time; behold, now is the day of salvation** (2 Cor. 6:2) [because after the Rapture will be a day of God's wrath, and not His grace]. Remember God has promised that only Israel will be saved out of it. And at that time, you do not want to gamble with eternity, especially if you're not a Jew of the flesh.

Now, I can hear your saying, "I don't think that is fair." NEWS FLASH! The Trinity will never consult with you regarding the Father's plan for Israel and the world. So stop trying to resist God. We all need Him, whereas, GOD has no needs, being the only Self-Existing One. **For you were bought with a price** [of Jesus dying for your sins on the cross]; **therefore glorify God in your body and in your spirit, which are God's** (1 Cor. 6:20). Trust Him today! Don't gamble with eternity.

BOOK OF LIFE

In chapter 2, I explained the two applications to better understand the Book of Life: Before the Rapture of the Church &After the Rapture of the Church.

We've now come to the "After the Rapture of the Church" application. In Daniel 12:1, the prophet describes, **"And at that time shall Michael stand up, the great prince which stands for the children of thy people: and there shall be a time of trouble, such as never was since there was a nation even to that same time: and at that time thy people shall be delivered, every one that shall be found written in the book"** [referring to the Raptured saints whom God snatched from the earth to avoid the 7-year period of the Tribulation and Great Tribulation on earth]. Thus the names of all human beings who missed the Rapture (1 Thes. 4:16, 17), and the names of all those who spurned the rule of Christ during the Millennium, were NOT found in the **book of life.** In horrifying shock, some of them will no doubt protest, **"Lord, Lord, have we not prophesied in thy name? And in thy name have cast out devils? And in thy name done many wonderful works? And then will I** (Jesus) **profess unto them, I never knew you: depart from Me, ye that work iniquity** (Matt. 7:22, 23).

CARNALITY VS. HYPOCRISY

Although shocking for some people, it should be of no surprise that the carnal Christian and the proud hypocrite share similar characteristics, but have one underlying distinction: The carnal Christian has "fire insurance", whereas the proud hypocrite DOES NOT HAVE FIRE INSURANCE. Because worldly thinking is wrong thinking, and even foolish (cf. 1 Cor. 3:19), the carnal Christian struggles to do God's will, whereas, the proud hypocrite is not interested in GOD or His will, but only self-promotion. The hypocrite lacks the one key ingredient for salvation --that being, **Christ in you, the hope of glory** (Col. 1:27b)]. Material gain and worldly acclaim are much more appealing to the hypocrite.

Hence the Devil's children usually get the best seats at most church services and houses of worship. Do you remember the parable of the wheat and tares?

Jesus told His disciples, **"the kingdom of heaven is likened unto a man which sowed good seed in his field: But while men slept, his enemy came and sowed tares among the wheat, and went his way. But when the blade was sprung up, and brought forth fruit, then appeared the tares also. So the servants of the householder came and said unto him, Sir, did not thou sow good seed in thy field? From whence then hath it tares? He said unto them, an enemy hath done this. The servants said unto Him, Wilt thou then that we go and gather them up? But He said, Nay; lest while ye gather up the tares, ye root up also the wheat with them. Let both grow together until the harvest: and in the time of harvest I will say to the reapers, Gather ye together first the tares, and bind them in bundles to burn them: but gather the wheat into my barn"** (Matt. 13:24-30).

Hence Jesus instructs His church to let the "saints" and "sinners" grow together as well as the "carnal" and the "hypocrite". But as a matter of church discipline, each congregation must immediately address any flagrant and open sin committed by those congregants who especially hold prominent positions. If there is no repentance, the church is instructed to remove the "cancer" before it affects the whole body.

In 1 Corinthians 5, we find a man [who holds a prominent position in the church] decides to marry and have sex with his stepmother. Rather than mourn, the congregants brag about it (vs. 2). In response, the Apostle Paul has to instruct the Corinthian Church concerning this incestuous jackal, **"In the name of our Lord Jesus Christ, when ye are gathered together, and my spirit, with the power of our Lord Jesus Christ, to deliver**

such a one unto Satan for the destruction of the flesh that
the spirit may be saved in the day of the Lord Jesus" (vss. 4,5).
Without question, this offender is a carnal Christian. As such,
Paul is not advocating to kill the man, but to excommunicate
him. Here **the destruction of the flesh** cannot mean that the
person could be brought to death. God does not want him
killed; He wants him restored. In Matthew 18:11-20, Jesus
provides clear instructions on how to handle the wayward lost
sheep and administer church discipline.

Now concerning carnality, suffice it to say, no one can move
from "natural" to "spiritual" without passing through "carnal".
That's why, **as newborn babes,** the carnal Christian must **desire
the sincere milk of the word, that he or she may grow thereby**
(1 Pet. 2:2) and **grow in grace, and in the knowledge of our
Lord and Savior Jesus Christ** (2 Pet. 3:18). While the seed of
God's word is sown, the carnal Christian's response is normally
akin to seeds which **"fell among thorns". And the thorns grew
up, and choked it, and it yielded no fruit** (Mark 4:7). Jesus
further explains, **"And these are they which are sown among
thorns; such as hear the word, And the cares of this world,
and the deceitfulness of riches, and the lusts of other things
entering in, choke the word, and it becomes unfruitful** (Mark
4:18,19), thereby causing the carnal Christian to continuously
live in error (Matt. 22:29).

And it so happens that over time the carnal Christians' erro-
neous lifestyle exacerbates, and is worsened by their destructive thinking: **For to be carnally minded is death; but to be
spiritually minded is life and peace. Because the carnal
mind is enmity against God: for it is not subject to the law**

of God, neither indeed can be. So then they that are in the flesh cannot please God. But ye are not in the flesh, but in the Spirit, if so be that the Spirit of God dwell in you. Now if any man have not the Spirit of Christ, he is none of His (Rom. 8:6-9).

So because of their distracted and destructive thinking, the carnal Christians lay a futile foundation: **For other foundation can no man lay that is laid, which is Jesus Christ. Now if any man build upon this foundation gold, silver, precious stones, wood, hay, stubble: Every man's work shall be made manifest: for the day** [of the judgment seat of Christ](cf. 4:5 & 2 Cor. 5:10) **shall declare it, because it shall be revealed by fire; and the fire shall try every man's work of what sort it is. If any man's work abide which he hath built thereupon, he shall receive a reward. If any man's work shall be burned, he shall suffer loss** [of reward]**: but he himself shall be saved; yet so as by fire** (1 Cor. 3:11-15).

The phrase **"so as by fire"** is a phrase that I actually believe uniquely refers to our purification process by the Holy Ghost as He removes "the dross" from our lives. **Take away the dross from the silver, and there shall come forth a vessel for the refiner. Take away the wicked from before the king, and his throne shall be established in righteousness** (Prov. 25:4-5). WOW! What two prophetic verses!

Here's another application that relates to how the Holy Ghost purifies every believer, including the carnal Christian. Remember when Jesus bodily rose from the dead, He returned to earth and joined two men walking on the road to Emmaus who were very distraught over the crucifixion of Jesus. Scripture explains that **their eyes were restrained so that they should not recognize Him** (Luke 24:16). As evening approached, they urged Jesus to remain with them. **And it came to pass, as He (Jesus) sat at meat with them, He took bread, and blessed it, and brake, and gave to them. And their eyes were opened, and they knew Him; and He vanished out of their sight. And they said one to another, Did not our heart <u>burn within us</u>** [alluding to the inspirational and purifying purpose of the Holy Ghost] **, while He (Jesus) talked with us by the way, and while He opened to us the scriptures** (vss. 30-32). Also, keep in mind that Jesus **counseled the church at Laodicea to buy of Him gold tried in the fire, that they may be rich** (Rev. 3:18a). And let's not forget what Job said: **"But He knows the way that I take: when He has tried me, I shall come forth as gold** (Job 23:10). Let's even consider Peter's comment: **Wherein you greatly rejoice, though now for a season, if need be, you are in heaviness through manifold temptations. That the trial of your faith, being more precious than gold that perish, though it be tried with fire, might be found unto praise and glory at the appearing of Jesus Christ** (1 Pet. 1:6,7). Lastly, we read another affirming scripture, Acts 14:22: **Confirming the souls of the disciples, and exhorting them to continue in the faith, and that we** (all believers in Christ) **must through much tribulation enter the kingdom of God** (Acts 14:22).

Thus all Christians [whether carnal or spiritual] undergo the purification process that only trials can accomplish, before entering heaven. Scripture is clear: **Yea, and all that will live godly in Christ Jesus shall suffer persecution** (2 Tim. 3:12). **If** we suffer, we shall also reign with Him: if we deny Him, He also will deny us (2 Tim. 2:12).

As pertaining to the hypocrite, just remember that they are play actors only. And according to Jesus, their reputation is one of inflicting suffering rather than enduring suffering. They will never stand in line and sign up for anyone's suffering program.

HOPE OF THE HYPOCRITE

Job 8:13 reveals, **"So are the paths of all that forget God, and the hypocrite's hope shall perish.** The hypocrites shun God's righteousness, seek to establish their own righteousness, and would teach others to do so as well (cf. Rom. 10:3). Most of us know that offerings, fasting, and prayer are all acts of worship that should be rendered to God. For the hypocrites, their acts of worship become acts of self-righteousness to gain admiration of others. And Jesus warns us not to pattern ourselves after them: **"Take heed that ye do not your alms** (charitable deeds) **before men, to be seen of them: otherwise ye have no reward of your Father which is in heaven. Therefore when you do a charitable deed, do not sound a trumpet before you as the hypocrites do in the synagogues and in the streets, that they may have glory of men. Verily I say unto you, they have their reward. But when you do a charitable deed, do not let your left hand know what your right hand is doing, that your charitable deed may be in secret; and your Father which sees in secret will Himself reward you openly. And when thou pray, you shalt not be like the hypocrites. For they love to pray standing in the synagogues and on the corners of the streets** (OSTENTATIOUSLY)**, that they may be seen by men. Verily,**

I say unto you, they have their reward [of only impressing others and attracting attention to themselves] (Matt. 6:1-5). It's one thing to be fooled; It's another thing to fool yourself.

God's Rebuke

After finally being rejected from the temple, **Jesus spoke to the multitude, and to His disciples, saying: The scribes and the Pharisees sit in Moses' seat** [a position of authority]: **All therefore whatsoever they tell you to observe, that observe and do; but do not do according to their works; for they say, and do not do. For they bind heavy burdens, and grievous to be borne, and lay them on men's shoulders; but they themselves will not move them with one of their fingers. But all their works they do to be seen by men. They make broad their phylacteries, and enlarge the borders of their garments. And love the uppermost rooms** (best VIP seats) **at feasts, and the chief seats in the synagogues, and greetings in the markets, and to be called of men, Rabbi, Rabbi. But you, be not called Rabbi: for one is your Master, even Christ; and you are all brethren. And call no man your father upon the earth: for one is your Father, which is in heaven. Neither be ye called master: For one is your Master, even Christ. But he that is greatest among you shall be your servant. And whosoever shall exalt himself shall be abased; and he that humble himself shall be exalted** (Matt. 23:1-12).

Jesus further accuses them **"for shutting up the kingdom of heaven against men: for they neither go in themselves, neither suffer** (or allow) **them that are entering to go in** (vs. 13). They **devour widow's houses** (extorting money from the helpless and bringing them into deeper debt and bondage), **and for pretense make long prayers** (vs. 14): **They compass** (travel) **sea and land to proselytize a Gentile to convert to Judaism, and when he is made, they make him twofold** (twice) **the child of hell than themselves** (vs. 15), **they swear by the temple** [with impunity and no punishment for their disrespect] **but whosoever shall swear by the gold** [in which they mostly covet] **of the temple, he is a debtor** (vs. 16)[bound by his oath].

Fools and blind! For which is greater, the gold, or the temple that sanctifies the gold? And whosoever shall swear by the altar, it is nothing; but whosoever swears by the gift that is upon it, he is guilty (obligated). **Fools and blind! Which is greater, the gift, or the altar that sanctifies the gift? Whoever therefore shall swear by the altar, swears by it, and by all things thereon. And whoever shall swear by the temple, swears by it, and by Him that dwells therein. And he that shall swear by heaven, swears by the throne of God, and by Him that sits thereon. Woe unto you, scribes and Pharisees, hypocrites! For ye pay tithe of mint and anise and cumin, and have omitted the weightier matters of the law, judgment, mercy, and faith: these ought ye to have done, and not to leave the other undone. You blind guides, which strain at a gnat, and swallow a camel. Woe unto you, scribes and Pharisees, hypocrites! For you make clean the outside of the cup and platter, but within they are full of extortion and excess. Thou blind Pharisee, cleanse first that which is within the cup and platter, that the outside of them may be clean also. Woe unto you, scribes and Pharisees, hypocrites! For ye are like unto whited sepulchers, which indeed appear beautiful outward, but are within full of dead men's bones, and of all uncleanness. Even**

so you also outwardly appear righteous unto men, but within you are full of hypocrisy and iniquity. Woe unto you, scribes and Pharisees, hypocrites! Because ye build the tombs of the prophets, and garnish (adorn) the sepulchers (monuments) of the righteous, And say, if we had lived in the days of our fathers, we would not have been partakers with them in the blood of the prophets. Wherefore you are witnesses unto yourselves, that you are the children of them that killed the prophets. Fill you up then the measure of your fathers' guilt. You serpents, you generation of vipers, how can you escape the damnation of hell? Wherefore, behold, I send unto you prophets, and wise men, and scribes: and some of them you shall kill and crucify; and some of them shall you scourge in your synagogues, and persecute them from city to city. That upon you may come all the righteous blood shed upon the earth, from the blood (murder) of Abel unto the blood (murder) of Zechariah son of Barachias, whom you slew between the temple and the altar (cf. 2 Chron. 24:20-21). Verily, I say unto you, All these things shall come upon this generation (Matt. 23:17-36).

Thus scripture is clear; Jesus is emphatic: NO HYPOCRITE WILL ENTER HEAVEN. Vengeance is mine, I will repay, says the Lord (Rom. 12:19b)-- especially at The Great White Throne of Judgment.

14

THE ETERNAL STATE / NEW HEAVEN & NEW EARTH (Rev. 21-22)

And I saw a (brand) **new heaven and a** (brand) **new earth: for the first heaven and the first earth were passed away** (cf. 20:11); **and there was no more sea.** Nearly three fourths of this present earth is covered by water. Every living thing [people, plants, animals, insects, vegetation—all things visible and invisible] requires water for its survival. And because of its water content, only planet earth can be inhabited. In Isaiah 45:18, scripture affirms, "For thus says the LORD that created the heavens; God Himself that formed the earth and made it, He created it not in vain, He formed it to be inhabited: I am the LORD; and there is none else." So to the few "smarter than God" billionaires who desire to set up shop on planet Mars, please leave all your wealth behind, because there's NO WATER ON MARS or any other planet. Again, GOD CREATED ONLY PLANET EARTH TO BE INHABITED. And I just saved the "smarter than God" rich folks, BILLIONS.

And I John saw the holy city, New Jerusalem (heaven's capital city), **coming down from God out of heaven, prepared as a bride adorned for her husband.** From a child, I've often heard the words: "Heaven is a prepared place for a prepared people." Here our marriage to the Lord Jesus Christ is finally consummated in heaven. While Jesus was on earth, He reminded us, "In my Father's house are many mansions (dwelling places): If it were not so, I would have told you [because Jesus does not go around telling lies]. I go to prepare a place for you. And If I go and prepare a place for you, I will come again and receive you unto Myself; that where I am, there you may be also" (John 14:2, 3).

On the former earth, we understand that no one could see God's face and live. In Exodus 33, we read, "Moses beseech God, show me thy glory. And He said, I will make all My goodness pass before thee; and I will proclaim the name of the Lord before thee; and will be gracious to whom I will be gracious and will show mercy on whom I will show mercy. And He said, thou cannot see My face and live. And the Lord said, Behold, there is a place by Me, and thou shalt stand upon a rock: And it shall come to pass while My glory passes by, that I will put thee in a cleft of the rock, and will cover thee with my hand while I pass by: And I will take away mine hand, and thou shalt see My back parts: but My face shall not be seen" (Ex. 33:18-23).

And I heard a great voice out of heaven saying, Behold, the tabernacle (and presence) **of God is with men, and He will** (personally) **dwell with them, and they shall be His people, and God Himself shall be with them, and be their God. And God shall wipe away all tears from their eyes; and there**

shall be no more death, neither shall there be any more pain:
Because death and pain cause crying, the new reality will be one
without death, pain or crying. As Paul reminds us, "Death is
swallowed up in victory" (1 Cor. 15:54). **For the former things**
(of disappointment, suffering, sorrow, disease, misfortune, and
any negativity) **are passed away. And He** (Jesus Christ) **that
sat upon the throne said, Behold, I make all things new. And
He said unto me, Write: for these words are true and faithful**
[because it's impossible for God to lie (Heb. 6:18) Again, God
is not a man, that He should lie; neither the son of man, that
He should repent. Hath He said, and shall He not do it? Or
hath He spoken, and shall He not make it good (Num. 23:19)?
And He said unto me, It is done. I am Alpha and Omega (the
first and last letters of the Greek alphabet), **the beginning and
the end** (cf. Isa. 44:6).

WATER OF LIFE

**I will give unto him that is athirst of the fountain of the water
of life freely** (without cost). In Matthew 5:6, Jesus promised,
"Blessed are they which do (spiritually) hunger and thirst after
righteousness: for they shall be filled. In Isaiah 55:1, the prophet
chimes in, "Ho, to everyone who thirsts, come you to the waters,
and he who has no money, come you, buy, and eat; yes, come,
buy wine and milk without money and without price." In John
7:37-38, we're reminded, "On the last day, that great day of the
feast, Jesus stood and cried out, saying, 'If anyone thirsts, let him
come to Me and drink. He who believes in Me, as the Scripture
has said, out of his heart will flow rivers of living water."

And do you remember the Samaritan woman at the well? Jesus, being wearied and tired from His journey, said unto her, Give Me a drink. For his disciples were gone away unto the city to buy food. Then said the woman of Samaria unto Him, How is it that You, being a Jew, ask drink from me, who is a woman of Samaria? For the Jews have no dealings with the Samaritans. Jesus answered and said unto her, If you knew the gift of God, and who it is who says to you, 'Give me a drink'; thou would have asked Him, and He would have given you living water. The woman said to Him, "Sir, You have nothing to draw with, and the well is deep. Where then do You get that living water? Are You greater than our father Jacob, who gave us the well, and drank from it himself, as well as his sons and his livestock?" Jesus answered and said to her, "Whoever drinks of this water will thirst again, but whoever drinks of the water that I shall give him will never thirst. But the water that I shall give him will become in him a fountain of water springing up into ever-lasting life" (John 4:6-14)

I believe the "water" in these passages speaks to the promise of the Holy Spirit. In John 3:3-5, Jesus tells Nicodemus, "Except a man be born again, he cannot see the kingdom of God." Nicodemus was puzzled and asked, "How can a man be born when he is old? Can he enter the second time into his mother's womb, and be born? Jesus answered, Verily, verily, I say unto you, except a man be born of water [natural birth] and of the Spirit [spiritual birth] (cf. 1 Cor. 15:44), he cannot enter the kingdom of God." It's only through the eyes of the Holy Spirit can a person see the Father/Son relationship; It's only through the eyes of the Holy Ghost can a personal see spiritual life [or life as it really is].

He that overcomes shall inherit all things; and I will be his God, and he shall be My son. Here John reminds us, "For whatsoever is born of God overcomes the world: and this is the victory that overcomes the world, even our faith. Who is he that overcomes the world, but he that believes that Jesus is the Son of God"?

THE OUTCASTS

But the fearful, and unbelieving, and the abominable, and murderers, and whoremongers, and sorcerers, and idolaters, and all liars, shall have their part in the lake which burns with fire and brimstone: which is the second death.

What a serious and dreadful warning to all the hell-goers! The Bible clearly identifies the unredeemed sinners in several passages of which I will share only four:

Because that, when they knew God, they glorified Him not as God, neither were thankful; but became vain in their imaginations, and their foolish heart was darkened. Professing themselves to be wise, they became fools. And changed the glory of the incorruptible God into an image made like to corruptible man, and to birds, and four-footed beasts, and creeping things. Wherefore God also gave them up to uncleanness through the lusts of their own hearts, to dishonor their own bodies between themselves. Who changed the truth of God into a lie, and worshiped and served the creature more than the Creator, who is blessed forever. Amen. For the cause God gave them up unto vile affections: for even their women did change the natural use into that which is against nature: And likewise also the men, leaving the natural use of the woman, burned in their lust one toward another; men with men working that which is unseemly (and shameful), and receiving in themselves that recompense (and penalty) of their error which was meet [due and fitting]. And even as they did not like to retain God in their knowledge, God gave them over to a reprobate mind, to do those things which are not convenient (fitting). Being filled with all unrighteousness, fornication, wickedness, covetousness, maliciousness; full of envy, murder, debate (strife), malignity (evil-mindedness); whispers, backbiters, haters of God, despiteful (violent), proud, boasters, inventors of evil things (including abortion pills), disobedient to parents, without understanding, covenant breakers, without natural affection, implacable (unforgiving), unmerciful: Who knowing the judgment of God, that they which commit such things are worthy of death, not only do the same, but have pleasure (approval) in them that do them (Romans 1:21-32).

Do you not know that the unrighteous will not inherit the kingdom of God? Do not be deceived. Neither fornicators, nor idolaters, nor adulterers, nor homosexuals, nor sodomites, nor thieves, nor covetous, nor drunkards, nor revilers, nor extortioners (blackmailers) will inherit the kingdom of God (1 Cor. 6:9-10).

Now the works of the flesh are evident, which are: adultery, fornication, uncleanness, lewdness, idolatry, sorcery, hatred, contentions jealousies, outbursts of wrath, selfish ambitions, dissensions, heresies, envy, murders, drunkenness, revelries, and the like; of which I tell you beforehand, just as I also told you in the past, that those who practice such things will not inherit the kingdom of God (Gal. 5:19-21).

But know this, that in the lasts days perilous times will come: For men will be lovers of themselves, lovers of money, boasters, proud, blasphemers, disobedient to parents, unthankful, unholy, unloving, unforgiving, slanderers, without self-control, brutal, despisers of good, traitors, headstrong, haughty, lovers of pleasure rather than lovers of God, having a form of godliness but denying its power. And from such people turn away! For of this sort are those who creep into households and make captives of "silly" gullible women loaded down with sins, led away by various lusts, always learning and never able to come to the knowledge of the truth (2 Tim. 3:1-7).

And there came unto me one of the seven angels (cf. Rev. 15:1) **which had the seven vials** (bowls) **full of the seven last plagues, and talked with me, saying, Come hither, I will show thee the bride, the Lamb's wife** [who will represent God's city, the New Jerusalem] (vs.9). She is the heavenly city referred to in Hebrews 12:22, whose builder and maker is God (Heb. 11:10) and prepared especially for her (Heb. 11:16). **And He carried me away in the spirit to a great and high mountain, and showed me that great city, the holy Jerusalem** [which has always existed in eternity], **descending out of heaven from God, Having the glory of God: and her light was like unto a stone most precious, even like a jasper** (diamond-like) **stone, clear and crystal** [radiant and pure]; To this description, the Psalmist expresses, "Out of Zion, the perfection of beauty, God hath shined (Ps. 50:2).

And had a wall great and high [to show its security and protection], **and had twelve gates** [to show its accessibility], **and at the gates twelve angels** [were stationed], **and names written**

thereon, which are the names of the twelve tribes of the children of Israel [to forever commemorate God's covenant relationship with Israel]: **On the east three gates; on the north three gates; on the south three gates; and on the west three gates. And the wall of the city had twelve foundations, and in them the names of the twelve apostles of the Lamb** [to forever commemorate God's covenant relationship with the church of which the apostles and the prophets are the foundation (Eph. 2:20)]. **And he that talked with me had a golden reed to measure the city, and the gates thereof. And the city lies foursquare, and the length is as large as the breadth: and he measured the city with the reed, twelve thousand furlongs** (1,500 miles cubed). **The length and the breadth and the height of it are equal. And he measured the wall thereof, a hundred and forty and four cubits, according to the measure of a man, that is, of the angel.** As John McArthur, Jr. simply puts it, "A yard is a yard, a foot is a foot, and a mile is a mile, whether for humans or angels." (The MacArthur New Testament Commentary, Revelation 12-22, p. 282). **And the building of the wall of it was jasper: and the city was pure gold, like unto clear glass. And the foundations of the wall of the city were garnished with all manner of precious stones. The first foundation was jasper** (diamond); **the second, sapphire** (blue stone); **the third, a chalcedony** (agate stone); **the fourth, an emerald** (green stone); **The fifth, sardonyx**(red and white striped stone); **the sixth, sardius** (blood-red stone); **the seventh, chrysolite** (yellow or gold stone); **the eight, beryl** (green stone); **the ninth, a topaz** (greenish gold stone); **the tenth, a chrysoprasus** (gold-tinted green stone); **the eleventh, a jacinth** (bluish purple stone); **the twelfth, an amethyst** (purple stone). Such a spectrum of dazzling colors, refracting the splendor of God's glory throughout the re-created universe, makes me want to stop putting up Christmas lights. Heaven's actual view will be a much more "far over the top" tremendous dazzling place to behold that one could ever imagine. According to 1 Corinthians 2:9, Eye has not seen, nor ear heard, Nor have entered into the heart of man The things which God has prepared for those who love Him.

And the twelve gates were twelve pearls; every several (single) **gate was of one pearl** [nearly 1,400 miles high]: Without question, these gigantic pearls will be an eternal reminder symbolizing Christ's "unequaled and immense" suffering on that "old rugged cross." **And the street of the city was pure gold, as it were transparent glass** [allowing the light of God's glory to blaze through]. **And I saw no temple therein: for the Lord God Almighty and the Lamb are the temple of it.** Here we're reminded, "Howbeit, the Most High does not dwell in temples made with hands, as the prophet says: Heaven is My throne, and earth is My footstool. What house will you build for Me? Says the Lord, Or what is the place of My rest? Has not My hands made all these things (Acts 7:48-50)? **And the city had no need of the sun, neither of the moon, to shine in it: for the glory of God** (The Father) **did lighten it, and the Lamb** (Jesus Christ) **is the light thereof.** To get a clearer understanding of this verse, just go outdoors on any bright sunny day. The brightness will represent the presence of God the Father, whereas, the sun will be the source of that day's brightness. In heaven, **the glory of God** the Father is the "Omnipresent, Intangible and Invisible" brightness, whereas, Jesus the Son, is its source. Scripture is very clear: No man hath seen (or never will see) God (The Father) at any time; the only begotten Son, which is in the bosom of the Father, He hath declared Him (John 1:18). And on that same note, scripture adds, "That thou keep this commandment without spot, unrebukable, until the appearing of our Lord Jesus Christ. Which in His times He shall show, who is the blessed and only Potentate, the King of kings, and Lord of lords; Who only hath immortality, dwelling in the LIGHT [which is in the bosom of the Father] which no man can approach unto; whom no man hath seen, nor can see: to whom be honor and power everlasting. Amen" (1 Tim. 6:14-16).

Now someone may say, "Ok, I get it. But I have one more question: WHERE IS THE HOLY SPIRIT?" Answer: He's inside of you and every other human citizen of heaven. Scripture explains, "But if the Spirit of Him that raised up Jesus from the dead dwells in you, He that raised Christ from the dead shall also quicken your mortal bodies by His Spirit who dwells in you (Rom. 8:11). Thus being in heaven will be the consummation of all things. Scripture reports, And we know that all things work together for good to them that love God, to them who are the called according to His purpose. For whom He (The Father) did foreknow, He also did predestinate to be conformed to the image of His Son, that He (Jesus) might be the first-born among many brethren. Moreover whom He did predestinate, them He also called: and whom He called, them He also justified, them He also glorified" (Rom. 8:28-30). Here I strongly encourage you to find your Bible, dust it off and read the last verses (31-39) of this amazing chapter while the youngsters use their smart phones.

And the nations of them which are saved shall walk in the light of it: and the kings of the earth do bring their glory and

honor into it (vs.24). This particular verse is the fulfillment of Isaiah 60:3 which proclaims, "And the Gentiles shall come to thy light, and kings to the brightness of thy rising. And to that end, we are no longer designated "kings and priests" as during the Millennium (cf. Rev. 1:6). In the Eternal State, every human citizen is a king, denoting absolute equality in heaven where every believer will be fully equal. There will be no class structure and no exclusive clubs. Everyone will be on the same level. **And the gates of it shall not be shut at all by day: for there shall be no night there.** This is because "the sun shall be no more thy light by day, neither for brightness shall the moon give light unto thee: but the Lord shall be unto thee an everlasting light, and thy God thy glory and the days of thy mourning shall be ended" (Isa. 60:19-20). **And they shall bring the glory and honor of the nations into it.** This is because "thy people also shall be all righteous: they shall inherit the land forever, the branch of My planting, the work of My hands, that I may be glorified. A little one shall become a thousand, and a small one a strong nation: I the Lord will hasten it in His time" (Isa. 60:21-22). **And there shall in no wise enter into it anything that defiles, neither whatsoever works abomination , or makes a lie:** [For violence shall no more be heard in thy land, devastation nor destruction within thy borders; but thou shalt call thy walls Salvation, and thy gates Praise] (Isa. 60.18). **but they which are written in the Lamb's book of life** (vs.27).

Chapter 22 continues: **And he showed me a pure river of water of life, clear as crystal, proceeding out of the throne of God and of the Lamb. In the midst of the street of it, and on either side of the river, was there the tree of life** (cf. Gen. 2:8-9; Gen. 3:22-24) to represent eternal sustenance and immortality,

which bare twelve manner of fruits, and yielded her fruit every month (developed and ripen for food).

Even though this is the eternal state and the four calendar seasons are time related, heaven's provisions are yet communicated in the familiar terms of time: **and the leaves of the tree were for the healing of the nations** (vs.2). Here Ezekiel explains, "And by the river upon the bank thereof, on this side and on that side, shall grow all trees for food, whose leaf shall not fade (or wither), neither shall the fruit thereof be consumed (or fail). It shall bring forth new fruit according to his months, because their "life-given" waters flow from the sanctuary: and the fruit thereof shall be for food, and the leaf thereof for medicine (Ezek. 47:12). Please remember that glorified bodies cannot get sick or experience starvation. The leaves will not treat illness, but (in this case) serve as vitamins to promote general health just like the fruit will be for enjoyment, and not sustenance.

And there shall be no more curse (cf. Gen. 3:17-19): **but the throne of God and of the Lamb shall be in it; and His servants shall serve Him. And they shall see His face** [and not be consumed by His blazing presence]; Again, John reminds us, "Beloved, now we are children of God; and it has not yet been revealed what we shall be, but we know that when He is revealed, we shall be like Him, for we shall see Him as He is (1 Jn.3:2). We're further reminded when GOD told Moses, "You cannot see My face; for no man shall see Me and live" (Exodus 33:20). **And His name shall be in their foreheads** (vs. 4) to show ownership and consecration (Ex. 28:36-38).

And there shall be no night there; and they need no candle, neither light of the sun; for the Lord God gives them light: Here verse 5 reminds us that God is light, and in Him is no darkness at all (1 John 1:5b). And when we are in His immediate presence, His glory makes all other sources of **light** unnecessary. As Zechariah puts it, "But it shall be one day which shall be known to the Lord, not day, nor night: but it shall come to pass, that at evening time it shall be light" (Zech. 14:17). The psalmist also explains, "For with You is the fountain of life; In Your light we see light (Ps. 36:9). **and they shall reign forever and ever** which will be the ultimate fulfillment of Daniel's prophecy: But the saints of the most High shall take(receive) the kingdom, and possess the kingdom forever, even forever and ever. Then the kingdom and dominion, and the greatness of the kingdom under the whole heaven, shall be given to the people, the saints of the Most High, whose kingdom is an everlasting kingdom, and all dominions shall serve and obey Him (Daniel 7:18, 27). In Revelation 3:21, Jesus reminded the church: To him who overcomes I will grant to sit with Me on My throne, as I also overcame and sat down with My Father on His throne. It's GUARANTEED!

Christ is to come quickly.

And He said unto me, These sayings are faithful and true; and the Lord God of the holy prophets sent his angel to show unto His servants the things which must shortly be done. Behold, I come quickly: blessed is he that keeps the sayings of the prophecy of this book.

Now we've come to the urgency of the moment. Inaction is an action that's certain to carry eternal consequences. For all rebels, both angels and humans alike have been cast into the lake of fire without a moment's relief. Then it will be forever too late for God-rejecting sinners to come to saving faith in Jesus Christ. In this verse, all believers (and especially ministers) are admonished not to shirk or deviate from **the sayings of the prophecy of this book** of Revelation simply because some will question its relevance or deny its authority. Paul faithfully reminds us, "We then, as workers together with Him, beseech you also that you receive not the grace of God in vain. [And some of us know the GRACE acronym all too well—**G**od's **R**edemption **A**t **C**hrist **E**xpense]. For He says, I have heard you in a time accepted, and in the day of salvation I have helped you. Behold, now is the accepted time, behold now is the day of salvation" (2 Cor. 6:1-2). "Whereas you do not know what will happen tomorrow. For what is your life? It is even a vapor that appears for a little time and then vanishes away" (James 4:14). "While it is said, TODAY IF YOU WILL HEAR HIS VOICE, HARDEN NOT YOUR HEARTS, AS IN THE PROVOCATION" [Rebellion](Heb. 3:15).

As ministers and believers, we are called not only to guard the scriptures, but also to obey them. Jesus clearly tells us, "If you love me, keep my commandments (Jn. 14:15). And hereby we do know that we know Him, if we keep His commandments. He who says, I know Him, and does not keep His commandments, is a liar, and the truth is not in him. But whoever keeps His word, truly the love of God is perfected in him. By this we know that we are in Him (1 Jn. 2:3-5). As believers, we should live as if Jesus could come at any moment. We should not get distracted by the world's condition. Jesus faithfully reminds us, "these things I have spoken unto you, that in Me you might have peace. In the world, you shall have tribulation: but be of good cheer; I have overcome the world (Jn. 16:33). Hence Christ's return will not be conditioned upon the decadence of society, but upon the spread of the gospel. For this very reason, God wants His people to always be solution-oriented, and NOT problem-oriented. WE WILL NOT BE RAPTURED UNTIL THE GOSPEL IS PREACHED IN ALL THE WORLD FOR A WITNESS UNTO ALL NATIONS.

"And this gospel of the kingdom shall be preached in all the world for a witness unto all nations; and then shall the end come (Matt. 24:14). The imminence of the Rapture is certain. Nonetheless, only GOD knows when the preaching of the gospel will have reached "every kindred, and tongue, and people, and nation" (Rev. 5:9b) in order to gather the 24 elders who represent the Raptured Church.

And I John [identifying himself] **saw these things, and heard them. And when I had heard and seen, I fell down to worship before the feet of the angel which showed me these things.** Of course, the apostle knew that we shouldn't worship angels (19:10. Nonetheless, John was simply overwhelmed in wonder and worship. **Then said he unto me, See thou do it not: for I am thy fellow servant, and of thy brethren the prophets, and of them which keep the sayings of this book: worship God** [because both angels and humans are all created servants of God]. And Colossians 2:18 reminds us, "Let no man beguile (defraud) you of your reward in a voluntary worship of angels, intruding into those things which he hath not seen, vainly puffed up by his fleshly mind."

And he saith unto me, Seal not the sayings of the prophecy of this book: for the time is at hand [and the return of Christ is imminent]. **He that is unjust, let him be unjust still: and he which is filthy, let him be filthy still: and he that is righteous, let him be righteous still: and he that is holy, let him be holy still.** This is because God's Word is the only thing that can change us. Your response to His Word will be your lot forever. Hence scripture warns, "TODAY IF YOU WILL HEAR HIS VOICE, HARDEN NOT YOUR HEARTS, AS IN THE PROVOCATION" [Rebellion] (Heb. 3:15).

And behold I come quickly [says Jesus]: **and my reward is with me, to give every man according as his work shall be** (1 Cor. 3:9-15; 2 Cor. 5:9-10). **I am Alpha** [origin and source of all things] **and Omega** [the goal and aim of all things] (cf. Rom. 10:4)], **the beginning and the end, the first and the last. Blessed are they that do His commandments, that they may have right to the tree of life** [denoting immortality and divine blessing (cf. 2:7, 22:2)], **and may enter in through the gates into the city** [having heavenly citizenship]. **For without** [outside the city and in the lake of fire (vs. 15; 21:8, 27)] **are dogs** (impure and malicious people) , **and sorcerers** [who practice witchcraft], **and whoremongers** [who practice all kinds of sexual immorality], **and murderers** [who often kill the innocent, including abortion providers], **and idolaters** [to include sun worshipers and tree huggers, **and whosoever loves and makes a lie** [including corrupt politicians]. **I Jesus have sent mine angel to testify unto you these things in the churches. I am**

the root and the offspring of David (cf. Isa. 11:1, Rom. 1:3, Rev. 5:5) **and the bright and morning star** (Num. 24:17; 2 Pet. 1:19). **And the** (Holy) **Spirit and the bride** [which is the church (cf. 19:7-9, ; 21:9)] **say, Come. And let him that hears say, Come. And let him that is athirst** [having a strong sense of spiritual need (cf. Isa. 55:1)] **come. And whosoever will** [choose salvation], **let him take the water of life freely.** THIS IS GOD's LAST CALL FOR SINNERS TO COME TO FAITH IN JESUS CHRIST.

For I testify unto every man that hears the words of this prophecy of this book, If any man shall add unto these things, God shall add unto him the plagues that are written in this book: Here God offers a clear warning against altering His word. **And if any man shall take away from the words of the book of this prophecy, God shall take away his part out of the book of life, and out of the holy city, and from the things which are written in this book.** And according to Deuteronomy 12:32, "Whatever I command you, be careful to observe it, you shall not add to it nor take away from it." This is a clear warning to anyone who would willfully distort the book of Revelation. Such people reveal that they are not genuine believers, and will experience "the wrath to come"(1 Thes. 1:10). **He which testifies these things says, Surely I come quickly. Amen. Even so, come, Lord Jesus. The grace of our Lord Jesus Christ be with you all. Amen.**

In summary, as we live in the hope of the Lord's return, scripture reminds us, "Knowing this first, that there shall come in the last days scoffers, walking after their own lust, and saying, where is the promise of His coming? For since the fathers fell asleep, all things continue as they were from the beginning of the creation" (2 Pet. 3-4).

Nonetheless, the answer to the world's problems is to be found in the return of Jesus Christ who is the sovereign Son of God. Don't delay. Trust Him as your personal Lord & Savior today!

Every sin that you have ever committed, whether past, present, or future, was imputed to Him and judged so that at this moment you can have eternal life. According to Roman 4:8, "Blessed is the man to whom the Lord shall not impute sin." Jesus has cleared your account and will never count your sins against you.

Eternal life is as close to you as your very own mouth: That if you confess with your mouth the Lord Jesus and believe in your heart that God has raised Him from the dead, you will be saved [from an eternal hell] (Rom.10:9).

May Grace be with you all. Amen (Heb. 13:25).

BONUS READING

What in Hell do you want?

And I say unto you my friends, be not afraid of them that kill the body, and after that have no more that they can do. But I forewarn you of whom you shall fear: Fear Him, who after He has killed, has power to cast into hell; Yes, I say unto you, Fear Him (Luke 12:4, 5).

Chained Forever
Then said the king to the servants, Bind him hand and foot, and take him away, and cast him into outer darkness; there shall be weeping and gnashing of teeth (Matt. 22:13).

Conscious Suffering
"For I am tormented in this flame" (Luke 16:24).

Continuous Burning
And if thy foot offend thee, cut it off: It is better for thee to enter life lame, rather than having two feet, to be cast into hell, into the fire that shall never be quenched (Mark 9:45).

Conviction of Memory
But Abraham said, Son, remember that in your lifetime you received your good things, and likewise Lazarus evil things; but now he is comforted and you are tormented (Luke 16:25).

Demons' Torture Chamber
Then shall He (Jesus) say to those on the left, Depart from Me, you cursed, into everlasting fire [which was] prepared for the devil and his angels.

Forever Descending
And the fifth angel sounded, and I saw a star fall from heaven unto the earth: and to him was given the key to the bottomless pit (Rev. 9:1).

Glimpse Paradise
And in hell he (the rich man) lift up his eyes, being in torments, and sees Abraham afar off, and Lazarus (the beggar) in his bosom (Luke 16:23).

God's Viewership
Hell is naked before Him, and destruction hath no covering (Job 26:6).

God's Wrath
For a fire is kindled in My anger, and shall burn unto the lowest hell; It shall consume the earth with her increase, and set on fire the foundations of the mountains (Deut. 32:22).

Hear Screams of Fellow Hell-Goers
And shall cast them into the furnace of fire: there shall be wailing and gnashing of teeth (Matt. 13:50).

Maggots' Feast
Where their worm does not die, and the fire is not quenched (Mark 9:48).

No Party Time
Then will I cause to cease from the cities of Judah, and from the streets of Jerusalem, the voice of mirth, and the voice of gladness, the voice of the bridegroom, and the voice of the bride: for the land shall be desolate [and a picturesque of hell] (Jer. 7:34).

No Sight of Fellow Hell-Goers
And cast the unprofitable servant into outer darkness: there shall be weeping and gnashing of teeth (Matt. 25:30).

Satan's Eternal Torments
And the devil that deceived them was cast into the lake of fire and brimstone, where the beast (Anti-Christ) and the false prophet are, and shall be tormented day and night for ever and ever (Rev. 20:10).

Sight of the Righteous
There shall be weeping and gnashing of teeth, when you shall see Abraham, and Isaac, and Jacob, and all the prophets, in the kingdom of God, and you yourselves thrust out (Luke 13:28) (cf. Luke 16:23).

Stench Untold

And they have built the high places of Tophet, which is in the valley of the son of Hinnon, to burn their sons and their daughters in the fire; which I commanded them not, neither came into My heart. Therefore, behold, the days come, says the Lord, that it shall no more be called Tophet, nor the valley of the son of Hinnon, but the valley of slaughter: for they shall bury in Tophet, till there be no place. And the corpses of this people shall be meat for the fowls of the heaven, and for the beasts of the earth; and none shall frighten them away (Jer. 7:31-33).

Commentary: "In the time of Jesus the Valley of Hinnon was used as the garbage dump of Jerusalem. Into it were thrown all the filth and garbage of the city, including the dead bodies of animals and executed criminals. To consume all this, fires burned constantly. Maggots worked in the filth. When the wind blew from that direction over the city, it's awfulness was quite evident. At night, wild dogs howled and gnashed their teeth as they fought over the garbage.

Jesus used this awful scene as a symbol of hell. In effect He said, 'Do you want to know what hell is like? Look at the valley of Gehenna.' So hell may be described as God's cosmic garbage dump. All that is unfit for heaven will be thrown into hell" (Nelson's Illustrated Bible Dictionary, year 1986, p. 473).

Unquenchable Thirst

And he (the rich man) cried and said, Father Abraham, have mercy on me, and send Lazarus (the beggar), that he may dip the tip of his finger in water, and cool my tongue; for I am tormented in this flame (Luke 16:24).

Various Torments

And in hell he lift up his eyes, being in torments, and sees Abraham afar off, and Lazarus in his bosom (Luke 16:23).

WHAT WILL WE DO IN HEAVEN?

Drink And he showed me a pure river of water of life, clear as crystal, proceeding out of the throne of God and the Lamb. In the midst of the street of it, and on either side of the river, was there the tree of life, which bare twelve manner of fruits, and yielded her fruit every month: and the leaves of the tree were for the healing of the nations (Rev. 22:1-2).

Eat And when one of them that sat at meat with him heard these things, he said unto him, Blessed is he that shall eat bread in the kingdom of God (Luke 14:15). And he said unto me, Write, Blessed are they which are called unto the marriage supper of the Lamb. And he said unto me, These are the true sayings of God (Rev. 19:9).

Enjoy eternal pleasures Thou wilt show me the path of life: in thy presence is fullness of joy; at thy right hand there are pleasures for evermore (Ps. 16:11).

Enjoy luxury and fellowship with Jesus In my Father's house are many mansions: if it were not so, I would have told you. I go to prepare a place for you. And if I go and prepare a place for you, I will come again, and receive you unto myself; that where I am, there ye may be also (John 14:2,3).

Experience paradise And Jesus said unto him, Verily I say unto thee, Today shalt thou be with me in paradise (Luke 23:43).

Explore the infinitely vast universe Speaking of GOD, He made the Arcturus (The Great Bear), Orion, and Pleiades, and the chambers of the south. He does great things past finding out, and wonders without number (Job 9:9-10). As the host (stars and galaxies) of heaven cannot be numbered, neither the sand of the sea measured (Jer. 33:22a).

Fellowship with Old Testament Saints And I say unto you, That many shall come from the east and west, and shall sit down with Abraham, and Isaac, and Jacob, in the kingdom of heaven (Matt. 8:11).

Judge angels Know ye not that we shall judge angels? How much more things that pertain to this life (1 Cor. 6:3) Note: The 12 apostles will judge the twelve tribes of Israel during the millennium only: And Jesus said unto them, Verily is say unto you, That ye which have followed me, in the regeneration when the Son of man shall sit in the throne of his glory, ye also shall sit upon twelve thrones, judging the twelve tribes of Israel (Matt. 19:28). "Regeneration" Ref. Romans 11:26 – And so all Israel shall be saved..

Learn For we know in part, and we prophesy in part. But when that which is perfect is come, then that which is in part shall be done away (I Cor. 13:9-10). Our knowledge will become exponential, but limited (like the angels). GOD alone is omniscient! Ref. 1 Peter 1:12).

Received by our Personal Welcoming Committee And I say unto you, Make to yourselves friends of the mammon of unrighteousness; when ye fail [die], they may receive you into everlasting habitations (Luke 16:9)

Rest And I heard a voice from heaven saying unto me, Write, Blessed are the dead which die in the Lord from henceforth: Yea, says the Spirit, that they may rest from their labors; and their works do follow them (Rev. 14:13).

Reunite with Loved Ones But now he is dead, wherefore should I fast? Can I bring him back again? I shall go to him, but he shall not return to me (2 Samuel 12:23). Please note: Our (saved) Loved Ones who predeceased us will return with Jesus at the rapture (cf. 2 Cor. 5:8). For if we believe that Jesus died and rose again, even so them also which sleep in Jesus will God bring with him (I Thes. 4:14).

Rewarded But when thou make a feast, call the poor, the maimed, the lame, the blind: And thou shalt be blessed; for they cannot recompense thee: for thou shalt be recompensed at the resurrection of the just (Luke 14:13,14).

Rule and reign with Christ And their shall be no night there; and they need no candle, neither light of the sun; for the Lord God gives them light: and they shall reign for ever and ever (Rev. 22:5).

See God's face and never forget names For now we see through a glass, darkly; but then face to face: now I know in part; but then shall I know even as also I am known (I Cor. 13:12). No introduction. No language barriers. But you have an unction from the Holy One, and you know all things (1 John 2:20).

Serve I saw in the night visions, and, behold, one like the Son of man came with the clouds of heaven, and came to the Ancient of days, and they brought Him near before Him. And there was given Him dominion, and glory, and a kingdom, that all people, nations, and languages, should serve Him: His dominion is an everlasting dominion, which shall not pass away, and His kingdom will be that which shall not be destroyed (Daniel 7:13,14). And there shall be no more curse: but the throne of God and of the Lamb shall be in it; and his servants shall serve Him (Rev. 22:3).

Sing Make a joyful noise unto the Lord, all ye lands. Serve the Lord with gladness: Come before His presence with singing (Ps. 100:1,2).

Watch the Horrors of Hell-Goers For as the new heavens and the new earth, which I will make, shall remain before me, says the Lord, so shall your seed and your name remain . . . And they shall go forth, and look upon the corpses of the men that have transgressed against me: for their worm shall not die, neither shall their fire be quenched; and they shall be an abhorring unto all flesh (Isaiah 66:22,24). Ref. Luke 16:26

Work But Jesus answered them, My Father has worked [even] until now, [He has never ceased working; He is still working] and I, too, must be at [divine] work (John 5:17) Amplified And whatsoever ye do, do it heartily, as to the Lord, and not unto men; Knowing that of the Lord ye shall receive the reward of the inheritance: for ye serve the Lord Christ (Col. 3:23,24).

Worship After this I beheld, and, lo, a great multitude, which no man could number, of all nations, and kindred, and people, and tongues, stood before the throne, and before the Lamb, clothed with white robes, and palms in their hands; And cried with a loud voice, saying, Salvation to our God who sits on the throne, and unto the Lamb. And all the angels stood round about the throne, and about the elders and the four beasts, and fell before the throne on their faces, and worshiped God, Saying, Amen: Blessing, and glory, and wisdom, and thanksgiving, and honor, and power, and might, be unto our God for ever and ever. Amen (Rev.7: 9-12).

BIBLICAL ANSWERS TO WORLD CONCERNS

Aliens Are there aliens on other planets? No. For thus says the Lord that created the heavens; God Himself that formed the earth and made it; He hath established it, He created it not in vain, He formed it to be inhabited: I am the Lord; and there is none else (Isaiah 45:18).

Angels Do I have a guardian angel? Yes. For He shall give His angels charge over thee, to keep thee in all thy ways. They shall bear thee up in their hands, lest thou dash thy foot against a stone (Ps. 91:11-12). Take heed that you do not despise one of these little ones, for I say unto you, that in heaven their angels do always behold the face of my Father which is in heaven (Matt. 18:10).

Character How do I "walk the walk?" Be not deceived: evil communications corrupt good manners. Awake to righteousness, and sin not; for some have not the knowledge of God: I speak this to your shame (I Cor. 15:33-34).

Climate Change While the earth remains, Seedtime and harvest, Cold and heat, Winter and summer, and day and night shall not cease (Gen. 8:22).

Confidence How can I get more confidence? For thus says the Lord God, the Holy One of Israel: In returning and rest shall ye be saved; in quietness and in confidence shall be your strength: and ye would not (Isaiah 30:15).

Dating Does God care if I date just anyone? Yes. Be ye not unequally yoked together with unbelievers: for what fellowship hath righteousness with unrighteousness? And what communion hath light with darkness (2 Cor. 6:14)? Wherefore putting away lying, speak every man truth with his neighbor: for we are members one of another (Eph. 5:25).

Disappointment Will God ever disappoint me? Let your conversation be without covetousness; and be content with such things as ye have: for He hath said, I will never leave thee, nor forsake thee. So that we may boldly say, The Lord is my helper, and I will not fear what man shall do unto me (Heb. 13:5-6).

Divorce Will God punish me for leaving my spouse? But if the unbelieving depart, let him depart. A brother or sister is not under bondage in such cases: but God hath called us to peace (I Cor. 7:15).

Evolution Through faith we understand that the worlds were framed by the word of God, so that things which are seen were not made of things which do appear [because nothing ever evolved over time] (Heb. 11:3).

Gender Male or female: Does it really make a difference? Yes. The woman shall not wear that which pertains unto a man, neither shall a man put on a woman's garment: for all that do so are abomination unto the Lord thy God (Deut. 22:5). Ref. I Cor. 6:9

Global Warming But the heavens and the earth, which are now, by the same word are kept in store, reserved unto fire against the day of judgment and perdition of ungodly men (2 Pet. 3:7).

GOD Has anyone seen GOD? No man hath seen God at any time; the only begotten Son, which is in the bosom of the Father, He hath declared Him (John 1:18). And He said [to Moses], Thou canst not see My face: for there shall no man see Me and live (Exodus 33:20).

Gossip What should I do when I hear gossip? Put away from thee a deceitful mouth, and perverse lips put far from thee (Prov. 4:24).

Heaven Who will go? For therefore we both labor and suffer reproach, because we trust in the living God, who is the Savior of all men, especially of those that believe (I Tim. 4:10).

Hell Who will go? The wicked shall be turned into hell, and all the nations that forget God (Ps. 9:17

Homosexuality Is homosexuality a sin? Yes. Thou shalt not lie with mankind, as with womankind: it is abomination (Lev. 18:22).

Hurricanes Does God cause them? And the same day, when the even was come, He (Jesus) said unto them, Let us pass over unto the other side . . . And there arose a great storm of wind, and the waves beat into the ship, so that it was now full . . . And He arose and rebuked the wind, and said unto the sea, Peace be still. And the wind ceased, and there was a great calm (Mark 4:35, 37-39). Hurricanes, tornadoes, tsunamis, earthquakes and all natural disasters occur because GOD cursed the earth: And unto Adam he said, Because thou hast hearkened unto the voice of thy wife, and hast eaten of the tree, of which I commanded thee, saying, Thou shalt not eat of it: cursed is the ground for thy sake; in sorrow shalt thou eat of it all the days of thy life (Gen. 3:17).

Ignorance Will God send anyone to hell who never knew Him or heard the gospel? But there is a spirit in man: and the inspiration of the Almighty gives them understanding (Job 32:8). That was the true Light, which lighted every man that comes into the world (John 1:9). For the invisible things of Him from the creation of the world are clearly seen, being understood by the things that are made, even His eternal power and Godhead; so that they are without excuse (Rom. 1:20).

Leadership Moreover thou shalt provide out of all the people able men, such as fear God, men of truth, hating covetousness: and place such over them, to be rulers of thousands, and rulers of hundreds, rulers of fifties, and rulers of tens (Exodus 18:21).

Love How will I know when I am in love? Love suffers long and is kind; love does not envy; love does not parade itself, is not puffed up; does not behave rudely, does not seek its own, is not easily provoked, thinks no evil; does not rejoice in iniquity, but rejoices in the truth (I Cor. 13:4-7).

Nationalism And (God) hath made of one blood all nations of men for to dwell on all the face of the earth [as national citizens, and not global citizens], and determined the times before appointed, and the bounds of their habitation (Acts 17:26).

Problems Is it possible to have a life without problems? No. Man that is born of a woman is of few days, and full of trouble (Job 14:1).

Religion Do all roads lead to God? Neither is there salvation in any other: for there is none other name under heaven given among men, whereby we must be saved (Acts 4:12) And as it is appointed unto men once to die, but after this the judgment (Heb. 9:27). Yes, all roads lead to God [as Savior or Judge], but all roads don't lead to heaven.

Stress Where is God when I'm stressed out? We are troubled on every side, yet not distressed; we are perplexed, but not in despair; Persecuted, but not forsaken; cast down, but not destroyed; Always bearing about in the body the dying of the Lord Jesus, that the life also of Jesus might be made manifest in our body (2 Cor. 4:8-10).

Terrorism They shall put you out of the synagogues; yes, the time is coming that whoever kills you will think that he's doing God service. And these things will they do to you because they have not known the Father nor Me (John 16:2, 3).

Trust It is better to trust in the Lord than to put confidence in man. It is better to trust in the Lord than to put confidence in princes [and politicians] (Ps. 118:8-9).

War If killing is wrong, is war also wrong? A time to love, and a time to hate; a time of war, and a time of peace (Eccl. 3:8). When it comes to good vs. evil, God is not neutral. The evil shall bow before the good; and the wicked at the gates of the righteous (Prov. 14:19). For he [government] is the minister of God to thee for good. But if thou do that which is evil, be afraid; for he bears not the sword [of capital punishment] in vain: for he is the minister of God, a revenger to execute wrath upon him that doeth evil (Romans 13:4).

Worry Is it ok to worry a lot? Be careful for nothing; but in everything by prayer and supplication with thanksgiving let your requests be made known unto God. And the peace of God, which passes all understanding, shall keep your hearts and minds through Christ Jesus (Phil. 4:6-7).

Worship When do I and how can I truly worship God? Give unto the Lord, O ye mighty, give unto the Lord glory and strength. Give unto the Lord the glory due unto His name; worship the Lord in the beauty of holiness (Ps. 29:1,2). But the hour cometh, and now is, when the true worshippers shall worship the Father in spirit and in truth: for the Father seeketh such to worship Him. God is a Spirit: and they that worship Him must worship Him in spirit and in truth (John 4:23, 24).

TOPICAL INDEX

ABOUT THE AUTHOR

Aaron Johnson is a husband, a father of four, and a grandfather of two. He has a host of relatives and cousins born from godly patriarchs and matriarchs who did not believe in abortion. He is a business manager/insurance agent who has taught the Bible for over 40 years. In 1988, Aaron received a BA in Religious Studies from Rice University. He's a former Asst. Pastor, a former Asst. Chaplain and a current Associate Minister who enjoys music (with gospel being his favorite). He loves to run, lift weights, shoot pool and enjoy a good movie. Being six feet tall, he slam dunked a basketball on a 10 ft. rim his last time, and one month before reaching age 41.

Such an achievement has nothing to do with bragging rights, but is simply giving to alert the reader that the content in this book is very candid and straight forward . . . and is written by a student athlete, and not a liberal academician.

Aaron is also the director of The America We Love Foundation. This is a Judeo-Christian Conservative website and organization that is known for promoting American traditional values.

CPSIA information can be obtained
at www.ICGtesting.com
Printed in the USA
LVHW091651211221
706849LV00001B/16

9 781662 834141